# Praise for *The Insider's Guide to Culture Change*

"If you are a leader who wants to build an enduring company where people go to work, are happy, and deliver exceptional results, read this book. It is filled with Siobhan McHale's 'insider' case studies and her groundbreaking four-step approach to culture change."
—Garry Ridge, Chief Executive Officer, WD-40 Company

"This book contains the most groundbreaking thinking on how to change workplace culture that I have seen in many years. Siobhan's methods will be transformational to unlocking culture change efforts across the world. This is a highly practical methodology from someone who has actually been through the process from the inside."
—Carolyn Taylor, Global Culture Change Pioneer and Author of bestselling *Walking the Talk: Building a Culture for Success*

"Culture is often regarded as a mystery. Yet this Pandora's box of myths and fallacies is critical to business performance. Through the expert eyes of Siobhan McHale, we clearly see how culture uniquely contributes to performance on every level. Whether you are a startup or an established international enterprise, you cannot afford to ignore this better, faster, easier way to enduring success."
—Richard Hames, Writer, Futurist, and Executive Director of the Centre for the Future

"Much wise advice and vital information from a master of organizational culture change."
—Richard Barrett, Founder of the Barrett Values Centre and the Academy for the Advancement of Human Values

"Siobhan brings a fresh voice based on deep experience; a luminary in the corporate culture conversation. *The Insider's Guide to Culture Change* is the perfect guide for anyone who wants to create a high performing and agile culture."
—David Hennessy, Host of *The Hennessy Report* podcast from Keystone Partners

"Culture is the operating system our companies run on. Those who ignore its tremendous power to drive business results do so at their peril. Siobhan McHale's book is an indispensable guide to making culture work for you rather than against you, and her four-step model to culture change is a vital tool for anyone seeking to make change happen at work."

—Aga Bajer, Culture Strategist,
Author, and *CultureLab* Podcast Creator

"If you're intrigued to find the big patterns that drive your culture and up for the hard work needed to shape them, this book is for you. Siobhan McHale will help you find the blend of know-how, true grit, and resilience you'll need for the task."

—Diane Smith-Gander,
Nonexecutive Director, Advocate for Gender Equity

"In today's ever-changing business environment, bad companies fold, good companies survive, and only great companies thrive and succeed. One of the secrets of greatness is undoubtedly the right culture. In this important book, Siobhan McHale provides readers with a no-nonsense formula for defining, creating, and maintaining the right culture, where people embrace change and agility that enables the organization to win. After all, organizations are neither agile nor innovative—only people are."

—Mihály Nagy, Founder of The HR Congress

"As CEO and chairman of major companies, I learned that how a company works is as important as what it does. Ensuring success is a function, not only in financial or market outcomes, but also through the creation of a high-energy performing organization with a vibrant culture, achieved through effective leadership and process. Siobhan's book offers pragmatic insight as to how to go about this."

—John McFarlane, CEO and Chairman of major companies

SIOBHAN McHALE

# THE INSIDER'S GUIDE TO CULTURE CHANGE

## CREATING A WORKPLACE THAT DELIVERS, GROWS, AND ADAPTS

HarperCollins
LEADERSHIP

An Imprint of HarperCollins

Published by HarperCollins Leadership, an imprint of HarperCollins Focus LLC.

Book design by Aubrey Khan, Neuwirth & Associates.

ISBN 978-1-4002-1466-2 (eBook)
ISBN 978-1-4002-1465-5 (HC)

Library of Congress Control Number: 2019945645

Printed in the United States of America
20 21 22 23   LSC   10 9 8 7 6 5 4 3 2 1

*To the leaders who embrace the challenges of culture change to create better workplaces.*

# CONTENTS

## · CHAPTER 1 ·
## LEARN THE INSIDER'S SECRET

## · CHAPTER 2 ·
## UNDERSTAND WORKPLACE CULTURE

# CONTENTS

## · CHAPTER 3 ·
## PREPARE FOR CHANGE

## · CHAPTER 4 ·
## DIAGNOSE THE CURRENT CULTURE

## · CHAPTER 5 ·
## REFRAME THE ROLES

# CONTENTS

## · CHAPTER 6 ·
## TAKE CHARGE OF THE JOURNEY

## · CHAPTER 7 ·
## ENGAGE THE ENTIRE ORGANIZATION

## · CHAPTER 8 ·
## ALIGN PROCESSES,
## POLICIES, AND PROCEDURES

CONTENTS

## · CHAPTER 9 ·
## GATHER CHANGE MOMENTUM

## · CHAPTER 10 ·
## CONSOLIDATE GAINS

# ACKNOWLEDGMENTS

Over my thirty-year career, many people assisted or mentored me as I gained the experience and expertise to write this book. A very special thanks to Michael Snell, a wonderful agent. He was willing to take a risk on a writer from Down Under, and he effortlessly bridged the sixteen-hour time difference between Truro, Massachusetts, and Melbourne, Australia. Michael walked with me every step of the way, provided invaluable input to the book, and he contributed greatly to the quality of the final manuscript. I appreciate his faith in me, and I feel very fortunate to have had the benefit of his talent, experience, and dedication in helping create this book.

A heartfelt thanks to everyone at HarperCollins Leadership for the opportunity to publish this book and their ongoing support. In particular, I'd like to thank Jeff James (Vice President and Publisher), Tim Burgard (Senior Acquisitions Editor), Hiram Centeno (Senior Marketing Manager), and Sicily Axton (Senior Publicity Manager). Thanks also go to Jeff Farr (Managing Editor) and Beth Metrick (Production Director) at Neuwirth & Associates, who expertly handled the editorial production of the book.

I have woven stories of inspirational culture leaders throughout this book. One of these leaders was John McFarlane, who was a privilege to work with over seven years at ANZ bank. He encouraged his employees to tap their true, authentic selves and create a "bank with a human face." Standing alongside John McFarlane were his team of capable and courageous executives who co-led the transformation to a more human bank—including (in no particular order) Sonia Stojanovic, Brian Hartzer, Peter Marriott, Graham Hodges, Alison Watkins, Louis Hawke, Elizabeth Proust, Bob Edgar, Elmer Funke Kupper, Peter Hodgson, Grahame Miller, Rick Sawers, Peter Hawkins, Greg Camm, Shane Freemen, David Boyles, Craig Coleman, Satyendra Chelvendra, Roger Davis, Chris Cooper, Gordon Branston, Carole Anderson, David Hornery, Ian Richard, John Winders, Bob Lyon, Peter McMahon, Bruce Bonyhady, Murray Horn, Mark Lawrence, Mike Grime, Steve Targett, Sir John Anderson, Rob Gousdswaard, Mike Guerin, and Brad Jordan.

I also thank my (Breakout) team at ANZ and the group of external facilitators who worked tirelessly to transform the culture at the bank. Special mention goes to my leadership group—Joanne Martin, Phillip Ralph, Chris Power, Mark Priede, and Rocco Cirillo—for their dedication. My gratitude also goes to Gita Bellin, a pioneer in the field of human transformation, who guided me on my higher journey toward becoming a culture change educator.

I wish to acknowledge the many leaders I have worked with over the years who have provided me with opportunities to deepen my culture expertise, including Robyn Brown, Reg Smith, Peter Goode, Graeme Hunt, Elizabeth Hunter, Stephen Phillips, and Diane Smith-Gander.

More recently, my leadership colleagues at DuluxGroup have demonstrated the real meaning of leader-led change and what it feels like to be part of a truly great culture. They include board members—Peter Kirby (ex-chairman), Graeme Liebelt (chairman), Andrew Larke, Joanne Crewes, Jane Harvey, and Judith Swales—and my executive team colleagues, Patrick Houlihan (MD and CEO), Stuart Boxer, Pat Jones, Martin Ward, Jennifer Tucker, Murray Allen, Richard Stuckes, Brad Hordern, Ian Rowden, and Simon Black. A special mention goes to my HR team at DuluxGroup for working alongside me as we continued to reinforce an engaged and high performing culture, including my leadership group of Luke Brabender, Sue Benefield, Lindy Visagie, Cassie Brain, Shaun Humphrey, Rebecca Cusack, Stephanie Watt, and Claudia Pernat.

A community of like-minded professionals provided regular feedback on my articles and videos on LinkedIn—they include Vitaly Geyman, Susan Franzen, Hilton Barbour, Denis Kelly, Jon Williams, Edwin Cohen, Karin

# ACKNOWLEDGMENTS

Volo, Brendan Geary, Luis Moura, Aga Bajer, Kristina Hiukka, Dr. Mervyn Wilkinson, Mark LeBusque, Christine Song, and Gene Bellinger. A special thanks goes to Peter Goral for his advice on branding and for being one of my most active supporters on LinkedIn. Thanks to Mihaly Nagy (founder of the HR Congress) and David Hennessy at Keystone Partners (and founder of the HR podcast *The Hennessy Report*) for being strong advocates and supporters of my work on organizational culture. Thanks also goes to Matthew Pollard for his feedback on the writing experience.

Close friendships have sustained me over the course of writing the book. I must thank Janice Gobey for listening to my ramblings about workplace culture over many cups of Earl Grey tea. I am grateful to Sonia Stojanovic, my former boss at ANZ bank, whose visionary leadership taught me that personal and organizational transformation go hand in hand. Angelica Fabian-Varga has been a friend over many years and always a great source of encouragement and energy. I met my longtime friend, Joan Lurie, when she joined my Breakout team at ANZ. She introduced me to the thinking of great systems practitioners Irving and Bella Borwick, whose approaches have influenced my work. In her own right, Joan is an authority in the field of systemic change. A special shout out goes to my friend and talented facilitator Greg O'Meara, who has also partnered with me over many years to transform workplace cultures.

My thanks also go to my partner, Trish, a fellow author, who planted the idea for this book many years ago over a glass of chardonnay at The Farmers Arms Hotel in Daylesford, Australia. Thanks for all your guidance and advice on the book direction and content—as well as for your love, support, and inspiration over the years. I could not have written this book without you.

Finally, my love and respect go to my parents, Patricia and Martin McHale, who encouraged my thirst for learning and gave me the gift of unconditional love. You are both gone too soon; I will miss you always.

## A SPECIAL INDUSTRY ACKNOWLEDGEMENT

I would like to acknowledge several thought leaders who have contributed greatly to the field of culture and who have influenced me in my work:

# ACKNOWLEDGMENTS

John Kotter, the change management guru and Konosuke Matsushita Professor of Leadership, Emeritus, at Harvard Business School, has been an inspiration to countless change practitioners all over the world. I want to thank John not only for his lifetime contribution to the understanding of change but also for influencing my life when he called me one day in 2005 to ask if he could feature my work as a case study at the Harvard Business School.

Edgar Schein has published extensively on the topic of culture and made a notable mark with his theories of organizational culture and leadership.

Carolyn Taylor, whose work I've admired for decades, provided another beacon in the change management field when she first came to my attention in 2005 with her groundbreaking book *Walking the Talk*. Carolyn has served as an inspiration and invaluable sounding board on my journey as an author.

Stan Slap, the author of several *New York Times* bestsellers on workplace culture, has been one of my inspirations in writing this book.

Thank you all for your ongoing contribution to the field of workplace culture and change.

Culture is always a work in progress, and no culture ever achieves perfection. During my research, I encountered many leaders who had embarked on culture change. Analyzing what they have done can help us on our own change journeys. They include (in alphabetical order):

- Ellyn Shook and Pierre Nanterme (Accenture)
- Brian Chesky, Nathan Blecharczyk, Joe Gebbia (Airbnb)
- Jeff Bezos (Amazon)
- Tim Cook (Apple)
- Michelle Moore and Brian Moynihan (Bank of America)
- Frank Wang (DJI)
- Patrick Houlihan (DuluxGroup)
- Jim Weddle (Edward Jones)
- Mary Barra (General Motors)
- Sundar Pichai (Google)
- Dharmesh Shah and Brian Halligan (HubSpot)
- Brad Smith (Intuit)

# ACKNOWLEDGMENTS

- Jean-Paul Agon (L'Oréal)
- Jørn Lyseggen (Meltwater)
- Kathleen Hogan and Satya Nadella (Microsoft)
- Reed Hastings (Netflix)
- The residents of Oulu in Finland
- Rose Marcario (Patagonia)
- Herve Humler (Ritz-Carlton)
- Gary C. Kelly (Southwest Airlines)
- Elon Musk (SpaceX)
- Daniel Ek and Martin Lorentzon (Spotify)
- Kevin Johnson (Starbucks)
- Team Sky
- Susan Chambers, Wanda Young, and Doug McMillon (Walmart)
- Jeffrey Raider, Andrew Hunt, Neil Blumenthal, and Dave Gilboa (Warby Parker)
- Garry Ridge (WD-40)
- Tony Hsieh (Zappos)

I hope the lessons from these leaders, contained in case studies in the book, can help you to learn more about culture, and continue to create workplaces that can deliver, grow, adapt, and prosper.

# PREFACE

## TWO LIFE-CHANGING MOMENTS

My name is Siobhan, pronounced *Shiv-awn* (Gaelic for Joan). I grew up in Ireland, in a big farmhouse surrounded by apple trees, with the River Inny running through the back field beyond the swaying cypress trees. My siblings and I played, fished, swam, and laughed our way through our childhood days. We spent so much time learning to play the piano, concert flute, drums, accordion, and tin whistle, singing and dancing the night away, that we jokingly called ourselves "the Irish von Trapps." I can still hear the sound of music.

Like so many kids of our generation, we did not appreciate the fact that our parents had not enjoyed such a carefree life. Nor did we appreciate all the sacrifices they had made to ensure so much joy and laughter for their kids. They also wanted to see us go out into the world and make a difference in the lives of others: "Keep learning, find your passion, see the world!"

I did see the world, leaving Ireland to study in England, and then jetting across the United States, Europe, and Asia for two big consulting firms before finally settling in Australia. Eventually, my parents moved Down Under to join their five children. They bought a house in Sydney's Sutherland Shire and soaked up the adventure, sunshine, and vibrant culture of their new homeland.

*The first life-changing moment:* Seven years after arriving in Australia, my mom was diagnosed with Lou Gehrig's disease. Before the disease stripped her of the ability to move, speak, or swallow, she and I went for a walk along Cronulla Beach. It was a cold, blustery winter's day, with dark grey clouds grazing the windswept headland. As we strolled along the sand, Mom kicked off her shoes and walked barefoot in the ebbing tide. I shivered as I joined her, linking arms and leaning my head against hers. We wended our way like a pair of coconspirators, sharing stories of those long-gone-by times on the farm in Ireland. When she asked me about my life now, I told her about my passion for helping people get the most out of their work lives. Her eyes lit up. "I just *knew* my children would make a difference in the world!" Eighteen months later, she passed away.

I share this story because I want my readers to know a little bit about who I am and why I wrote this book. At the risk of sounding corny, I really did want to fulfill my parents' wishes and do something meaningful and fulfilling with my life. I wanted to toss my own little pebble of difference into the big pond and watch the ripples carry people into workplaces where they could express their passion, find fulfillment, and make their own difference in the world. I began my journey by studying psychology, earning my bachelor's at the National University of Ireland in Galway on the west coast of Ireland. While my fellow young psychologists went on to pursue careers in mental health, I chose a different path. I had developed a keen interest in that one-third of a person's life spent working for a living. My colleagues devoted themselves to the other two-thirds, and I dove into the world of work, enrolling in a master's degree program in occupational psychology at the University of Sheffield in northern England. That degree helped me secure positions as a consultant at two of the largest consulting firms in the world.

I spent the next decade travelling across the United States, Europe, Australia, and Asia, helping leaders change and improve their workplace cultures. Along the way, I observed the subtleties and complexities of a subject so many leaders find baffling and hard to grasp. I watched toxic team environments drain the energy from employees and leave customers feeling angry and frustrated. And I witnessed high-performing, productive cultures bring out the best in their people and delight their customers with spectacular service. I loved it. I knew I'd found my purpose.

One evening, shortly after I learned of my mum's diagnosis, I was waiting in a taxi stand at Chicago's O'Hare International Airport when the temperature had dropped to seven degrees Fahrenheit. I realized I had hit a wall in my career. I had enjoyed my time at the global management consulting firm

Accenture, but I was not finding the work truly engaging anymore. It felt too much like more of the same old exploration of the same old ideas and theories about culture change. Suddenly, I longed to settle down, roll up my sleeves, and actually *do* culture change.

As a consultant, I had whisked in and out of clients' offices, but I had never felt that I had really put my own skin in the game. I yearned for a deeper connection to the work and the people I wanted to help. I wanted to trade Ms. Outsider's formal pinstriped business suit for Ms. Insider's comfortable cotton slacks and blazer, getting my hands dirty actually *using* the change tools I had developed over the past decade. Waiting for a taxi in the razor-sharp wind slicing off Lake Michigan, I decided to make a career U-turn.

Over the next two decades, I joined a series of large, international companies as the executive in charge of business transformation. This insider role gave me a different perspective to the journalists, academics, and consultants who were writing on the subject. I was no longer advising about change, I was now responsible for the change. I was standing side-by-side with leaders on a daily basis, helping them to transform the business.

I recall one of my most challenging and satisfying insider jobs at the Australia and New Zealand Banking Group Limited, commonly called ANZ. Originally recruited by the visionary change leader Sonia Stojanovic, I became head of transformation when Sonia left the bank three years later. In that position, I managed a team of change specialists who worked with the leaders who were striving to change the organization's culture.

When I came aboard, ANZ's culture was in disarray. Its customers were dissatisfied, its employees dreaded coming to work, and sagging revenues and profits had demoralized its leaders. While ANZ's executive team knew that they needed to instigate a turnaround, everything they tried only seemed to make matters worse.

It didn't take long for me to see what was really going on in the organization. Quite simply, it had lost the trust of the community. A complete lack of transparency on fees and all-too-frequent branch closures had damaged the bank's reputation. How ironic that an obsession with the bottom line had actually *damaged* the bottom line! Needless to say, ANZ's thirty-two thousand employees shared the community's negative view of their employer. Loyalty and trust had all but evaporated.

Over the course of the next seven years, our team of change specialists worked with John McFarlane and ANZ's leaders to implement the radical transformation I will detail later in this book.

But I'll share the punch line: In the end, ANZ went from the lowest performing financial institution in the country to the number one bank globally on the Dow Jones Sustainability Index. I had discovered the work that I found truly engaging.

*Then a second life-changing moment:* I was sitting in my office at the bank headquarters in Melbourne, Australia, when I got a phone call from John Kotter, the renowned Professor of Leadership who was at that time the foremost authority on the subject of managing change. I had read all Professor Kotter's books on change management and greatly admired his work. Why on earth would this titan of scholarship be calling *me*?

Well, it turned out that Kotter was looking for good stories about successful change he could use as case studies in his Harvard MBA class. Word of the remarkable culture transformation at ANZ bank had reached his ears, and he wanted to learn more about it. Long story short, Professor Kotter selected my recounting of the initiative as a prime example of engineering a successful culture transformation. I realized at that moment that my work was bigger than the company I was working for, and that it could benefit others.

The ANZ experience, along with three decades spent researching, analyzing, and applying new ideas in the field led me to write this book. In *The Insider's Guide to Culture Change,* I share the knowledge I have gained over many years as I addressed firsthand the fundamental factors that can create a workplace culture that delivers, grows, and adapts. The book is designed to help successful leaders continue to be successful, assist those leaders struggling with specific culture issues within organizations, and help those leaders facing fundamental workplace culture challenges in their businesses. My views and approaches often shatter the prevailing myths about transformation. In this book I offer a step-by-step guide that can make the change journey easier and quicker. I hope my approaches can help you on your own change journey and in creating a workplace that can deliver, grow, adapt and continue to prosper. And, as my mother always hoped, it might also be a lot more fun.

# THE INSIDER'S GUIDE TO CULTURE CHANGE

# 1

## LEARN THE INSIDER'S SECRET

### The Culture Disruptor

Few scandals in the history of business rival the 2001 collapse of Enron, the American energy company whose culture of greed and rapaciousness tumbled it from the pinnacle of success to the abyss of failure. Its leaders' unethical and illegal behavior resulted in one of the largest bankruptcies in American history and triggered the dissolution of Arthur Andersen, one of the top accountancy firms in the world.

During the Enron trial, the company's CEO, Jeffrey Skilling, maintained his innocence. These claims withered in the glare of the public spotlight. Testimony during the trial revealed Enron's involvement in a shocking number of illegal and underhanded schemes, including the firm's role in perpetrating an electrical energy crisis in California, in which blackouts and soaring bills resulted from Enron's manipulation of the energy supply. Enron even took power plants offline in order to make more money.

All this occurred despite the company's sixty-four-page *Code of Ethics*. The document, widely circulated online, detailed the company's values, including, believe it or not, integrity. Oh, Enron had maintained a strict policy of integrity over the years, if you define integrity as an adherence to a policy of greed and corruption. Unethical behavior ran from the C-suite all the way down to Enron's middlemen buying and selling electricity on the floor of the commodity exchange.

This case illustrates the fact that you cannot legislate a strong, positive, vibrant, corporate culture. What, exactly, do we mean by *corporate culture*? Every executive I've ever met uses the term, but I've found few who can clearly and concisely define it. My definition of workplace culture is *"The patterns or agreements that determine how the business operates."* A simplified version that I commonly use is: *"It's how things work around here".* No published policy can create a corporate culture. No document outlining an organization's bedrock values can guarantee that people will faithfully practice those values. Culture emerges not from a proclamation or code of ethics but from how people, especially the organization's leaders, behave day in and day out. As the sad story of Enron proves, it's possible for even the most honest and upright worker to get ensnared in, and corrupted by, a bad culture.

### A bad culture can corrupt good people.

In today's hyperconnected world of instantaneous global communication, massive market disruptions, the expansion of an all-powerful urban consumer class, conflicts within the multigenerational workforce, and increasingly strict laws and regulations governing corporate behavior in some countries, it takes more than pretty words to instill the values that will successfully steer a company through volatile and uncertain times.

A report by Aaron De Smet, "Culture can make or break agility," published on February 26, 2018, by McKinsey & Company, underscores the pressing need to build and maintain a good culture in turbulent times: "Only 4 percent of survey respondents have completed an organization-wide transformation.... The No. 1 problem they cite is culture." Another study, "2016 Global Human Capital Trends," by Marc Kaplan, Ben Dollar, and Veronica Malian, published by Deloitte on February 29, 2016, reports that "the impact of culture on business is hard to overstate" and that an overwhelming 82 percent of eleven thousand survey respondents in business leadership roles believed that culture is a source of competitive advantage.

If you want a high-performing, agile, market-dominating company that gets results no matter what challenges it faces, you'd better create a culture that will get the job done. Simple enough, right? No. Actually, it's a *whole* lot easier said than done. To paraphrase Louis Gerstner, the former chairman and CEO of IBM, turning a bad culture into a good culture is like teaching a herd of elephants to dance.

## UNDERSTANDING THE POWER OF CULTURE

During my first year at university, studying psychology in the seaside city of Galway on the west coast of Ireland, I could not find a summer job in that recession-plagued coastal region. Desperately in need of funds, I decided to take the boat over to London for the summer, hoping to find a job there. By a stroke of luck, I landed a position in a warehouse in north London, where I filled orders from music stores for vinyl records, those dinosaurs of the recording industry that are making a comeback today.

On my first morning in the warehouse, Emma, the team supervisor, instructed us to set off at a brisk pace, filling record orders as rapidly as possible. However, at morning tea one of my coworkers took me aside and told me (in a rather threatening tone): "You'd better slow down. If you work that fast, the boss will expect us all to do the same!"

Uh-oh! I was doing my job too well? That possibility had never dawned on me. My coworker had given me a clear message to slow down or risk the ire of my colleagues. But it was in my nature to always do my best. Well, nature won out in the end. I kept doing the best I could.

Two days later, Emma called me into her tiny office. I sat perched on a rickety chair as she fidgeted with her pen and told me, "Unfortunately, Siobhan, I don't have enough work here to keep you on, so we're going to have to let you go." As I looked around the bustling warehouse and thought about the backlog of customer orders, I could not believe my ears.

Only later, as I learned more and more about the nuances of corporate culture, did I realize that I lost the job, despite my best efforts, simply because I had operated outside the acceptable norms of that warehouse culture. I had not followed the unwritten rule that a worker should proceed at an orderly and tortoise-like pace. There was no room there for a hare!

Every culture, good, bad, or exceptional, exerts tremendous power in the workplace. A bad culture like the one at the music warehouse generates lackluster results. A corrupt culture like the one at Enron courts disaster while a good one ensures that employees perform to the best of their ability even when no one is watching. But people *do* watch! In today's hyper-connected world, evidence of a company's culture can go viral in a heartbeat. United Airlines learned this the hard way.

On Sunday, April 9, 2017, police officers forcibly removed a passenger from United Airlines flight 3411, breaking his nose in the process after he refused to give up his seat on an overbooked flight from Chicago to Louisville. When passengers' smartphones captured the event in all its bloody glory, it immediately went viral, drawing more than 210 million internet viewers within a matter of days.

The video evidence suggested that United Airlines cared more about its own welfare than that of its passengers. As it turned out, the company wanted to remove Dr. David Dao from the flight in order to make room for a United Airlines' employee who needed to get to another assignment. What sort of culture would do that? Not a customer-friendly one. Ironically, according to *Fortune*, the incident eventually wiped $1.4 billion off the company's market value.

*Culture can make or break your strategy.*

In the end, United Airlines was forced to reexamine and alter certain elements of its culture. All companies should do the same, and they should do it often. A bad culture will leak value from your business, drop by corrosive drop, and it can get quite ugly in one social media posting. Even a good culture can, over time, lose its power to keep a company at the top of its game. It's all about careful reinvention, making important alterations before that one costly mistake hits YouTube.

Culture differentiates one company from another. Think of it as an organization's personality, the set of unique attributes that give it life, make it stand out from the crowd, and give it an edge over its rivals; or, in the case of an Enron or my summer employer or a United Airlines, it can undermine an organization's ability to create and sustain a competitive advantage.

## SEIZING THE ULTIMATE COMPETITIVE ADVANTAGE

If your company makes widgets, your competitors can copy your product or even disrupt your market share with something that makes your widgets obsolete. You may jump on every management theory that comes along, from Lean Six Sigma, business process reengineering, total quality management, management by objectives, and benchmarking to knowledge management, e-business, economic value-add, big data, etc., etc., etc. You'll find a lot of company there. But no one can easily copy your company's culture. This explains why all those executives surveyed by pollsters cite it as a major priority.

This makes culture change one of the greatest untapped sources of performance improvement in organizations. If you get the culture right, the results will follow. Leaders who focus on the conditions that produce success (the culture) stand a far better chance of delivering the outcomes they desire.

*If you take care of the culture,*
*results will take care of themselves.*

You can picture culture at the hub of a multispoked wheel. It drives the way your employees design, research, and manufacture your goods; it influences how you move, sell, and service your products; and it dictates how you meet the expressed and unexpressed needs of your customers. Culture provides the key not only to today's success in those critical areas, but also to tomorrow's continued dominance in the marketplace. Manage it, or it will manage you.

Workers in every department spend a significant chunk of their lives on the job, whether in a high-tech startup in the Silicon Valley, a venerable insurance company in London, or a sprawling toy factory in Yiwu, China. The culture can either engage them to perform to the best of their abilities, or it can give them excuses for always falling short of the mark.

The human capital and management consulting company Aon Hewitt, in its report titled "Wired for engagement" published in November 2017, found that organizations with highly engaged workforces achieve measurably better business revenue outcomes. In short, highly engaged cultures, where employees feel inspired to strive for better results, get better results.

Annemarie Mann and Jim Harter, in a Gallup report "The Worldwide Employee Engagement Crisis" published January 7, 2016, reveal that a staggering 87 percent of employees worldwide are not engaged at work. The Gallup researchers found that, in the United States, only 32 percent of employees feel motivated to go the extra mile in the workplace. In other words, some 86 million full-time workers in the United States do not bring their best selves to their jobs.

What can leaders do to turn that around? They can construct and maintain a vibrant culture where people *choose* to bring their best selves to their work. This became especially important when the so-called millennials entered the workforce. This new generation did not want merely to come to work, punch the clock, go through the motions, punch the clock again, and go home. They wanted meaning and purpose in their jobs. The best cultures bestow that meaning and purpose.

That's the good news. Here's the bad news: building a great culture takes courage to begin the change and true grit to continue.

*Culture change is the hardest work you will ever do.*

I once worked with a colleague named Mal Ward, and admired his achievements over his career as a top executive. Mal always displayed the wisdom and humility of a truly great leader. Mal asked to meet with me, not long after he had been diagnosed with terminal cancer, to discuss the progress of culture change, at a company where he was serving as the chairman—a change effort that I had been helping to shape.

During our discussion in the high-ceilinged foyer of a Sydney hotel, Mal grew pensive as he shared memories of the high points of his life as a business leader. He singled out his role as CEO of a major telecommunications company: "That was the toughest but most rewarding job I've ever done, Siobhan. We contributed to the everyday lives of Australians by introducing mobile phone technology, but the biggest challenge was to prepare our people for the transition into a more competitive marketplace. That culture work was the most meaningful work of my career."

Mal died three months after our conversation, but I still recall his parting words that day: "Keep going with the culture building, Siobhan. It is the hardest work you will ever do, but it makes all the difference." Mal understood that culture building taxes leaders more than all of their other work combined. It makes budgeting and forecasting and strategic thinking look like middle school playground games. It takes both state-of-the-art technical management skills and best-in-class leadership capabilities to get the job done.

Sadly, however, a McKinsey report published in April 2015 and titled "How to beat the transformation odds," reveals that up to 70 percent of corporate change initiatives fail to deliver expected benefits. Throughout this book, I will detail many case studies where well-intentioned leaders embarked on a major culture change initiative they hoped would happen overnight, only to find it moving at the speed of a glacier and often with far-less-than-hoped-for results. You will learn why the popular conventional approaches simply do not work. And more important, I will offer a new methodology that I have developed, not as an outside consultant but as an insider charged with making culture change happen. It boils down to activating what I call The Culture Disruptor.

•   •   •

## ACTIVATING THE CULTURE DISRUPTOR

When John McFarlane was appointed CEO of the Australia and New Zealand Banking Group Limited (commonly known as ANZ), he walked into a storm. Banks across Australia had lost the trust of customers and the broader community. The growing complexity of its products, mysterious new fees, and branch closures in rural areas had invited so much public contempt that bank bashing had become a national sport with politicians, community groups, unions, churches, media, and radio hosts.

McFarlane would need to shake things up if he was going to win back trust in all the communities ANZ served. What must he do to transform this large organization from a hated enterprise to a widely admired institution? How could he engage the bank's thirty-two thousand employees to create a more people-friendly and customer-centered culture? In the end, it took seven years of hard work, but McFarlane eventually achieved his goal, turning his company into one of the top performing banks in the world.

How do leaders like John McFarlane create such remarkable change? Over the course of my thirty-year career I've analyzed successful (and unsuccessful) change efforts and I've come up with The Culture Disruptor—a four-step model that anyone can use to transform workplace culture. The Culture Disruptor, and the supporting analysis in this book, is designed to help successful leaders continue to be successful, assist those leaders struggling with specific culture issues within organizations, and help those leaders facing fundamental workplace culture challenges in their businesses.

The Culture Disruptor describes the four steps in successful culture change: *Diagnose* what's really going on, *Reframe* the roles, *Break* the patterns, and *Consolidate* the gains (illustrated in Figure 1.1).

This simple but powerful model captures the essence of the culture change process that we'll explore in detail throughout this book. Let's take a quick look at how The Culture Disruptor works, by using the ANZ as an example—one of the most successful culture change efforts I've been involved in.

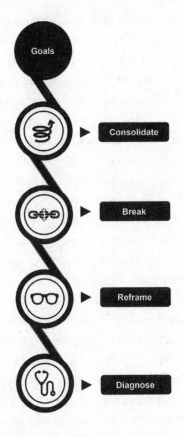

Figure 1.1. The Culture Disruptor

## DIAGNOSING WHAT'S REALLY GOING ON

The first step on The Culture Disruptor is to *Diagnose* what really going on, (this step is depicted by a stethoscope icon in Figure 1.1). Let's look at how this step played out in the ANZ transformation that I was intimately involved in from the early 2000s, that created the "bank with a human face." (In 2019, the findings of a Royal Commission enquiry into Australian banking would reveal the return of a toxic and greedy culture within the banking industry—but we'll come to how that happened later.) The company's visionary change leader, Sonia Stojanovic, had initially brought me aboard as the head of culture projects at the bank. Three years later, I stepped into her position as head of ANZ's transformation program (known as Breakout). When I first joined the bank, I found that while members of ANZ's executive team knew that they needed to do something to turn around low employee morale, widespread customer dissatisfaction, and sagging revenues and profits, they had not achieved the results they needed with a series of restructuring initiatives. In fact, matters had only gotten worse.

The consulting firm of McKinsey & Company had diagnosed a range of issues the company needed to resolve. My own investigations confirmed what was really going on in the organization: its people's behavior had cost ANZ the trust of both its customers and the wider community. The bank had received complaints about a lack of transparency when it came to customer fees and charges. The closure of banks in rural areas had also sparked anger and damaged ANZ's reputation in the community.

John McFarlane faced a daunting task the day he walked into ANZ's banking headquarters to begin his tenure as the company's CEO. ANZ, like all the other major banks in Australia, had earned a reputation as a greedy and insensitive institution. Writer Nicholas Way, in his *Business Review Weekly* article (January 25, 2001), "The Price of Bank Bashing," summed it up nicely: "Fee increases or branch closures cause a great public outcry in which any rational explanation from the banks is ignored, ridiculed or dismissed. They have become corporate pariahs." Way cited a survey of customer views on banking by the Financial and Consumer Rights Council that proved his point. Australians hated their banks.

McFarlane resolved to turn that attitude around. But where should he begin? A true turnaround in public perception would mean fundamentally changing the beliefs and behavior of ANZ's thirty-two thousand employees, and that would take more than a fancy new mission statement and a slick public relations campaign.

The new CEO decided to take a surprising first step in what eventually turned into a seven-year campaign to restore faith in his company. He would simply *listen* to the complaints of the bank's customers, shareholders, employees, and community stakeholders. Too often, those voices had fallen on deaf ears. His listening initiative made a good impression. It showed the naysayers that he sincerely wanted to understand their concerns. For the first time in a long time, the bank was showing the world a human face. As he met with a wide range of unhappy Australians, he made it clear that the company's mission went far beyond satisfying investors with handsome returns. The bank, he insisted, would not rest until it met or exceeded the needs and expectations of *all* its stakeholders.

Behind the scenes, we were working feverishly to figure out the underlying issues. We found that a deeply embedded dysfunctional pattern was driving it all. Decisions about almost everything, even the day-to-day customer experience in the branches, came from on high. This meant that frustrated customers often waited weeks to get answers to even the simplest questions and concerns.

Of course, the employees who actually dealt with customers every day felt they couldn't exercise any initiative to solve problems. So, who was accountable for the bank's bad reputation? The "order givers" in the head office blamed branch staff. The "order takers" on the front lines pointed the finger at the head office. And around and around it went, with customers getting more confused and angrier every day. We decided that nothing would change until we dealt with this basic blame game.

## REFRAMING ROLES

The second step on The Culture Disruptor is *Reframe* the roles, or see the work through a different lens—depicted by a pair of glasses in Figure 1.1. First, let me explain what I mean by "roles." I believe that the roles we play in life and at work influence our behavior just as powerfully as our personality. Take "Sarah Connors," for example. She wakes up on Monday morning, hugs her husband, Mark, and bounds out of bed to get their nine-year-old twins ready for school. Chatting about the day ahead with Mark, she fulfills the role of loving wife. Pouring milk into the twins' cereal bowls and checking for any symptoms of the flu, she fulfills the role of parent.

Ninety minutes later, Sarah steps onto the train and settles into her usual seat before opening her laptop to review the day's schedule at Mount Sinai Hospital in New York, where she works as head of the cardiology department. She loves her role as a team leader. On her morning rounds, Sarah talks with a group of first-year medical students, comfortably switching into her role as teacher. Later in the morning, she catches up with her boss to discuss the need for new imaging equipment in her department, and she effortlessly takes up the role of negotiator. When a colleague whisks into her office late in the day to ask her opinion about a troubling diagnosis, Sarah steps into the role of advisor.

Imagine how Sarah's behavior shifts as she moves into all the different roles she must play each day. By nature a rather quiet and reserved woman, she adjusts her behavior in ways that make her effective in each role. She doesn't talk to her family the same way she talks with students, patients, colleagues, or her boss. How does Sarah manage to shift her behavior seamlessly across all her interactions with so many different people? She holds in her mind's eye a map that guides and shapes her behavior. This mental map influences how she performs a given role.

Sarah doesn't let her personality dictate her behavior. This may seem like a fairly obvious point, but most leaders believe that personality governs human actions and that traits such as extroversion, introversion, shyness, gregariousness, dominance, and submissiveness rule an individual's behavior. In fact, a whole army of trainers and consultants in the field of change management preach this sermon. "Figure out personality types, then change them to support your transformation initiative." I think that's the hard way to do it. It's far easier, I believe, to accept people for who they are and work, instead, on reframing the role they need to play in whatever culture change you have initiated.

Leaders who work with and change how people frame their roles can accelerate organizational change. Rather than trying to change people's personalities, they work to reframe the way people think about and take up their roles in the change effort.

*Modify the role, not the person.*

John McFarlane understood that employees in the bank branches felt like order takers who waited for the order givers in the head office to tell them what to do. He needed to reframe their role from "order takers" to "service givers" responsible for meeting the needs of customers. This reframing brought about rapid change with less noise in the organization.

Acting on the belief that organizations don't change, people's behavior does, the CEO invited each and every one of ANZ's employees to behave like leaders, or, to put it another way, to step into leadership roles that would help him build a more human, customer-centric culture. He summed up his expectation with a constant clarion call: "You must lead and inspire each other." He realized that to change the organizational culture, you must start by reframing the people's roles and mobilizing them to contribute to the change objectives.

McFarlane began that process by sending more than thirty-two thousand people on a program that would reframe their roles and equip them with the specific skills they needed to create this new culture. As they learned how to build better relationships with one another and their customers, they gained self-confidence and pride and much higher levels of customer satisfaction.

Their new relationship-building skills enabled them to replace the blame game with a sense of their own role in solving problems. This new take-charge-and-solve-the-problem mentality gradually transformed the workplace from a toxic and highly political work environment into one where people took initiative and worked together more effectively. Staff began to embrace the idea of turning the bank into a more human and caring place to work and do business. They took to heart the idea that they "bring their whole selves to work" and to think and act in a more emotionally intelligent way with colleagues and customers. No longer did customers wait, stewing, for a delayed and often confusing answer to a concern. No longer did employees dread coming to work. They felt engaged with their colleagues, their managers, and their customers.

McFarlane led by example and stuck to his promises. He refused to shut down any more branches in rural Australia, a bottom-line tactic that had become a lightning rod for customer anger about callous bankers caring more about their own profits than customers' welfare. Internally, he acted on his belief in developing talent by installing a Learning Centre in the heart of Melbourne's CBD (central business district). The center became a symbol of his commitment to his people and to creating a vibrant workplace where people could grow and seize opportunities for advancement. On a personal level, the CEO displayed his own more human side by playing his guitar at staff events and singing some of his favorite tunes, including The Animals' "House of the Rising Sun." That earned him the joking nickname "Holly-wood John."

John skillfully reframed his role when necessary from top boss to vision-ary leader, change champion, customer advocate, colleague, and musician. Reframing roles is an important step toward bringing about change faster and with minimum disruption in the workplace, because—like trying on a new pair of glasses—it enables people to look at the world through different lenses and to shift the way they think about and do their jobs.

At ANZ bank, people looked through a lens that showed them the power of the mandate to "lead and inspire each other." McFarlane called on every person in the bank to take up the role of "inspiring leader." This call to action engaged employees in successfully creating a "very different bank."

## BREAKING OUT OF DEEPLY EMBEDDED PATTERNS

Old cultures, like old habits, are hard to break. Implementing The Culture Disruptor's third step, *Break* the pattern (depicted by a broken chain in Figure 1.1.), John McFarlane oversaw a bank-wide restructuring effort he called "Restoring Customer Faith." The project's title highlighted the num-ber one problem ANZ needed to solve.

To tackle the old head office versus the branch network blame game that had so alienated customers and the community at large, the bank's leadership team introduced a new operating model that reframed the roles of the warring factions and focused them on cooperation and joint accountability: "We work together to serve the customer." Note how "We" replaced "us versus them."

The new operating model, designed to replace the old habit of pointing the finger at others for causing the bank's number one problem, placed cus-tomers at the heart of everything the bank did. Now, everyone would take joint accountability for meeting customer needs while still delivering on fi-nancial imperatives (that good old bottom line).

Take, for example, the story of Ella, the ANZ bank teller. One day she fielded a call from Tim, a long-standing customer. Tim told Ella that he was so excited about his upcoming trip to South America that he had forgotten to pick up the replacement ANZ credit card he had ordered after his had been stolen. "Ella, I can't get to the bank. The traffic's horrendous. My wife and I will be late for our flight!"

Ella stepped in to his rescue. She calmed Tim's frazzled nerves, hopped in a cab, and raced to Tim's doorstep, where she handed him his brand-new card. "Thank you, Ella! You've got a customer for life!" That's one moral of the story: delighting a customer. But the cultural moral was just as important: an employee feeling empowered to make a decision at the drop of a hat. Goodbye "order taker," hello "problem solver."

Change came about because head office staff had abandoned their old role of "order givers" in favor of one in which they functioned as "support providers." They became business partners responsible for providing branch staff with risk management, financial, and human resources (HR) services. In ANZ's seven hundred branch offices, workers like Ella stepped into their new roles of "problem solver" and "customer service provider." It took time for the new habits to take hold, but within a few years the new culture had made major strides toward making ANZ one of the most admired and successful banking institutions in the world.

## CONSOLIDATING GAINS WITH THE CULTURE DISRUPTOR

Over the course of the next seven years, I worked with ANZ's leaders to implement a radical transformation at the bank. The bank's executives knew that deeply embedding the new culture into the very fabric of the organization would require constant effort and vigilance over the long term, which is the fourth step on The Culture Disruptor, *Consolidate* the gains, (depicted as an upward spiral in Figure 1.1). McFarlane and his leadership team continued to introduce initiatives that added momentum to the change journey, including a volunteer community service program that gradually regained the trust of local communities.

ANZ's community service program allowed bank employees to take a paid leave of absence in order to participate in community service projects. In one particularly touching instance, a team from ANZ's Risk Department decided to use their volunteering leave to remove rubbish from a local beach during Clean Up Australia Day. After spending the day filling plastic bags with trash, they encountered a middle-aged man and woman walking along the sand. The bankers chatted with the couple, ultimately revealing that they worked for ANZ. That delighted the couple to no end. "What a caring bank!" Later, they told their family and friends about the encounter. One small act of community service dropped a pebble into the pond of public opinion and made big waves for the company's reputation.

After a lot of hard work and no end of patience and perseverance, we did get the results we needed at ANZ. I analyzed the change success at ANZ (and other organizations), which led me to develop The Culture Disruptor. By following this model's four basic steps, you can break out of the old ways to create a culture that delivers, grows, and adapts. McFarlane did just this when he led the transformation of ANZ from the lowest performing financial institution in the country to the number one bank globally on the Dow Jones Sustainability Index. Within seven years, profits more than doubled, with a share price nearly triple its earlier low point. ANZ was winning awards for leadership, employee engagement, and customer service. The firm had also become a magnet for talent, receiving more than ten thousand applications annually for its 250 graduate positions. Employees *loved* working at ANZ. Customers loved doing business there.

In an article that appeared in *The Australian,* April 27, 2001, titled "Lame Duck Bank Is Flying High," Mark Westfield gave McFarlane high marks: "Yesterday's 18 percent first half profit leap vindicates McFarlane's unique plan among his peer banks of eschewing traditional growth strategies and recasting the culture of his bank to lift efficiency and earnings. Three and a half years ago ANZ was the worst performer of the big banks, regarded as the highest risk bank investment by the market, and in strategic disarray." He went on to praise the CEO for inspiring his people to "work harder and work smarter." This, he informed his readers, "has turned ANZ from the industry lame duck into a highly polished money-making machine with an eye to its customer needs."

Leaders can follow ANZ's success, by activating The Culture Disruptor, and I will explore the model's four steps in more detail throughout this book.

## · POINTS TO REMEMBER ·

- The right culture can help a business to seize the ultimate competitive advantage.
- The Culture Disruptor helps to bring about successful transformation faster and with less noise.
- The first step on The Culture Disruptor is to *Diagnose* what's really going.
- The second step on The Culture Disruptor is to *Reframe* the roles.
- The third step on The Culture Disruptor is to *Break* the patterns.
- The fourth step on The Culture Disruptor is to *Consolidate* the gains.

# 2

## UNDERSTAND WORKPLACE CULTURE

### Debunking the Myths About Culture

Several years ago, I flew into Las Vegas for a leadership conference where two high-profile business leaders would deliver keynote addresses. I was excited to hear what they had to say. Sitting in the packed auditorium, I listened to them describe the changes they had overseen in their two different organizations. Slowly it dawned on me that neither executive fully grasped the basics of workplace culture.

The first speaker, the CEO of an engineering company, told us how he had launched his company on the path to becoming a high-performing, agile organization. Defining culture as "the values and behaviors at work," he concluded that the effort was still a work-in-progress. The second presenter, the head of a large department in the armed forces, shared his dream of replacing a male-dominated culture with one that embraced diversity and inclusiveness. He defined culture as "the stories people tell in the workplace." In the end, however, he admitted that, despite strong public support for the change, women in his organization were still suffering under a range of bullying and discriminatory practices, which the media had gleefully reported. The change effort had not eliminated harassment and intimidation within the ranks.

Despite the most admirable intentions, both change initiatives failed to get the desired results, because the leaders had not understood the fundamentals of workplace culture. As I sat on the plane home, I began to suspect that a lot of other leaders find it hard to change their organization's culture because they share those two speakers' misconceptions about how culture really works. After all, few leaders have received formal training in the subject and can therefore fly by the seat of their pants when it comes to implementing culture change. As a result, they end up doing it by trial and error, an approach that can prove costly and even disastrous.

Many years studying the phenomenon uncovered a surprisingly widespread myth about workplace culture: If you state the values you want your people to practice, they will automatically alter their behavior accordingly.

That's nonsense!

## BUSTING THE BIG MYTH
## ABOUT WORKPLACE CULTURE

Consider the case of my old friend "Jonathan Cohen," a colleague from my days as a management consultant. He had climbed the ladder to become a partner in "AAA," a big consulting firm that specialized in corporate restructuring and major IT initiatives. Jonathan had invited me to lunch to ask my advice about a problem that was plaguing his team's performance. "We've lost a lot of contracts lately. When I took a hard look at the reasons we're getting hammered by our competitors, I discovered that clients think we're stodgy, old school. I get it. We need to become innovation leaders."

With a flourish, he pulled a colorful brochure from his briefcase. Titled "Our Values," it listed what he thought described an innovative culture. "Be creative, push the envelope, think outside the box," and so forth. He frowned. "It's not working. I know that values drive behaviors, so I expected this brochure to engage my people. Now I can't figure out why it's fallen on deaf ears. The last presentation we made to a huge client prospect flopped because to them it was just same old, same old consultant-speak. Of course, we lost the gig."

I nodded, understanding his dilemma. "Forget about values and behaviors for a minute. We need to talk about what really drives culture."

"OK," he said. "But before we get into that, please, what the heck *is* culture?"

Good question. And one that too many leaders fail to ask. Over the past thirty years I have regularly asked executives to define "culture," and I have heard everything from, "It's the soft, fuzzy people stuff" to "It's how we do things around here."

I explained to Jonathan, a common definition I use, "Culture is how things work around here or how the place functions. It affects every aspect of your business, from how you develop solutions to how you sell your products or services to how you make your customers happy. It's all about patterns of thinking and relating that tell people how to behave in an organization. And these patterns start to take hold the first day that people walk into the workplace."

"I see," said Jonathan. "And all along I've been thinking culture is just about behaviors and values, when it's actually more about these patterns. But how do I change them and move culture in the right direction?"

This question marked the beginning of Jonathan's journey toward building a new culture at AAA. Before he or any other leader takes one step toward changing an organization's culture, he or she must grasp the basic understanding of its true nature. Sailors learn the sailing basics before they embark on a sea voyage. The captain must ensure that crew members understand, for instance, the difference between 'port' and 'starboard' before setting sail. Otherwise he puts the ship at risk of crashing or not reaching the end destination. Leaders must also grasp the culture basics before they embark on the change journey.

As I have pointed out, one popular belief holds that culture boils down to explicit values and behaviors. However, that assumption can get you into a lot of trouble. No matter how hard you try to change a culture by promoting new values ("Be bold! Be innovative!"), and then expecting your people to immediately embrace those values and alter their behavior accordingly, little, if anything, will change. To create true and lasting change, you must concentrate on the three key elements of workplace culture.

## FOCUSING ON THE THREE
## KEY ELEMENTS OF CULTURE

One afternoon a week after our first discussion, Jonathan Cohen and I stood at the whiteboard in his office at AAA Consulting. I began to draw The Culture Disruptor with a box next to it titled "Three elements of culture" (Figure 2.1). I explained to Jonathan, "You must focus on three key elements of culture in order to accelerate change—Mental Maps, Roles, and Patterns."

Jonathan nodded, "That's news to me, but I'm keen to find out more."

Like Jonathan, leaders must learn about and leverage these three key elements in order to successfully change workplace culture.

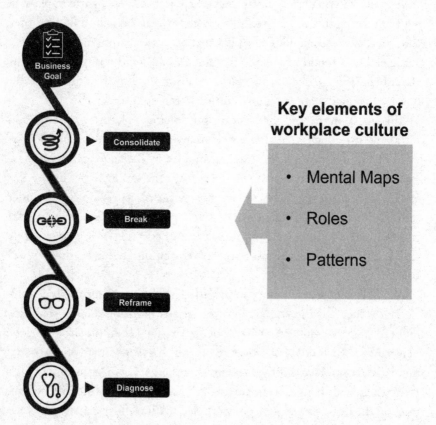

Figure 2.1. The Three Key Elements of Workplace Culture

Here is a description of each element:

- *Mental Maps:* The perceptions, point-of-view, and images you hold in your head about your work.
- *Roles:* The part played by a person (or function) in a given situation.
- *Patterns:* The (often hidden) agreements and cocreated rules between the parts.

Jonathan and I spent the rest of the afternoon exploring these three elements of culture in more detail.

## REDRAWING MENTAL MAPS

I began by drawing Jonathan's attention to the first element of culture, "We carry around mental maps in our heads that help us make sense of the world. The maps include our expectations, thoughts, feelings, assumptions, values, beliefs, and needs. The mental maps that people hold may not be visible to anyone else, but they strongly influence how people think and feel about their work and the roles they take up."

> *Mental maps influence how people*
> *see and take up their roles.*

Jonathan nodded. "So people won't knock on my door to explain their deepest feelings about the changes I want to make. But I can't expect much change if I do not deal with the hidden beliefs and assumptions that influence how they do their work."

"Exactly!" I replied. "Mental maps are like the GPS in your car; they help you navigate your way in the world. They contain information about the various roles that you step into throughout the day, and they work fine, but sooner or later they can become outdated. You may need to download the latest information about the roles you expect people to take up to ensure that they don't get lost during times of upheaval. Never forget that culture change can be a big upheaval."

Actions happen in our head before we perform them in the external world. An architect sees a beautiful house in her mind's eye before she sets pencil to paper. A basketball player imagines the ball swishing through the hoop before he throws it from the three-point line. A consultant pitching a proposal to a potential client rehearses it before she presents it in a meeting. A smart leader carefully thinks through a change initiative before she does anything to implement it.

I reinforced this point with Jonathan. "During culture change, you must help people redraw the mental maps that guide their role, so they can better navigate the change."

Jonathan tapped his marker on the whiteboard and mused, "I reckon my team members think that if they keep their heads down, all this talk about change will eventually fall by the wayside and they can get back to the comfort of doing their job the way they have always done it."

"Yes. You want different results, right? Getting different results depends on your ability to shift these mental maps and enable people to take up a different role."

## TAKING UP THE RIGHT ROLES

I pointed at the second element of culture (Roles) on the diagram, "The next element is role, the roles people play in doing their work. The role that your consultants have traditionally taken up may conflict with the way you want them to behave in a more innovative culture at AAA."

*Different results depend on taking up a different role.*

Jonathan got that point immediately. "I'm under a lot of pressure to hit my revenue targets, and I'm hearing rumors that some partners are questioning my recent promotion. I've tried everything from that values brochure to designing an open-floor workspace to encourage creative team interactions. I even sent my team to an innovation seminar. But nothing has changed. We're still the old stodgy bunch we always were."

I recognized Jonathan's dilemma. All leaders face the same challenge. How do you get people to do the right thing when you're not there to make sure they do? The leaders at Southwest Airlines solved that dilemma by inviting its people to take up the role of "servant leaders" when it came to meeting customer needs. This role framing had such a powerful impact that it led one Southwest employee to take such dramatic action, the story appeared in *Time* magazine. A passenger urgently needed to fly from Los Angeles to Denver to the aid of his daughter, whose live-in boyfriend had severely beaten her three-year-old son. As the grandfather dashed to Los Angeles International Airport, his wife explained the emergency to a Southwest agent, who passed the information along, eventually reaching the pilot.

Doctors had placed the injured boy in an induced coma and had told family members that he would not recover from his injuries. The boy's mother had decided to take her son off life support that evening in order to donate his organs to twenty-five people whose names were on waiting lists for transplants. "My husband wants to see his grandson one last time before that happens."

En route to the airport, the grandfather found himself mired in traffic. He would not make it to the terminal in time. He finally reached the airport, but he despaired. Surely the plane had departed by then. When he rushed to the gate, however, he could not believe his eyes. There on the tarmac stood the plane to Denver, its pilot patiently awaiting his arrival.

When the grateful grandfather thanked the pilot for his kindness, the pilot nodded and said: "The plane can't go anywhere without me, and I wasn't going anywhere without you. Now relax. We'll get you there. And again, I'm so sorry for your troubles."

Why did the pilot do that? It turned out that Southwest's culture included more than its famous commitment to on-time performance. The role that Southwest's people were expected to take up was that of "servant leader" who would always put customers' needs first. No boss told the pilot to do it. The role that he adopted in the culture told him to do it.

Jonathan knew the story, and he got my point about the relationship between role and results. "I get it! I can see that the consultants on my team are taking up the role of 'traditional thinkers,' which is keeping us stuck in the old ways of doing things."

"That may well be the case," I said, "but the role the consultants are taking up is connected to the pattern of relating in the culture. This brings us to the third key element of culture: the patterns that lie at the heart of workplace culture. Nothing will change until you fully understand and disrupt the existing patterns."

## DISRUPTING THE PATTERNS

I drew Jonathan's attention to the third key element of culture (Patterns) on the diagram.

"The third element is the deeply embedded patterns in the workplace. These are the unwritten rules that can capture people as soon as they enter the workplace. People come and go from any organization, but the patterns remain pretty much the same. You must look below the surface to discover these invisible patterns."

To show him what I meant, I asked several questions about the way Jonathan's team had always operated. Then I sketched a diagram of the old pattern of behavior at AAA (Figure 2.2).

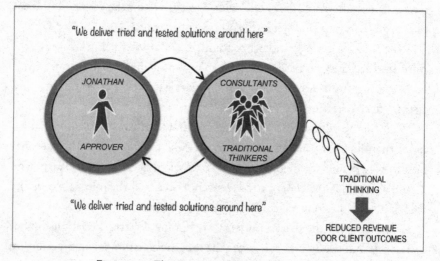

Figure 2.2. The Pattern of Traditional Thinking

Of course, Jonathan had approved his team's latest failed proposal. "You're acting as an enabler," I told him. "You espouse the values in your brochure, but your actions do not support the declared values. When you approved a lackluster proposal, you just fueled the old pattern. 'Tried and tested' is hardly innovative."

The "tried and tested" pattern had become deeply embedded over many years because it accounted for much of AAA's success in landing important clients who wanted to trust their futures to safe hands during major restructuring and IT projects. Jonathan had discovered, however, clients now wanted more agile and innovative solutions.

> *When the business environment changes,*
> *you must change with it.*

Jonathan saw my point about enabling the old pattern. "I'm co-creating the lack of innovation in my team."

I smiled. "Yes! And that means you can't blame *them* for failing to offer innovative solutions. It starts with *you*. You can disrupt the pattern by shifting your role from 'approver' to 'innovation leader.' That will trigger a shift in your people's behavior and a switch in *their* role from 'traditional thinkers' to 'innovative thinkers.'" I quickly sketched another diagram (Figure 2.3).

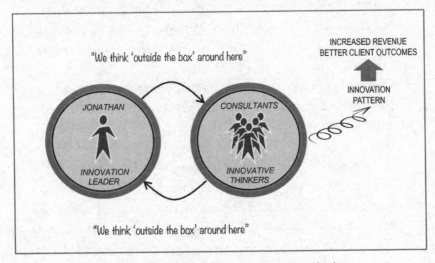

Figure 2.3. The New Pattern of Innovative Thinking

Jonathan's eyes widened. "Aha! I need to shift the cocreated pattern, not just the individual behaviors!"

"Spot on!"

Jonathan was beginning to see the need to shatter the big myth that culture is primarily about explicit values and behaviors. Culture, he realized, was less about *what* happened (the behaviors) and more about *how* the workplace functioned (the patterns)—these patterns held the key to lasting change.

## UNDERSTANDING PATTERNS
## AT A DEEPER LEVEL

What do I mean by patterns? They are the overriding, often unwritten rules that govern how people relate to one another and do their work. They share three characteristics:

1. **Hard to detect:** Sometimes formally stated, but quite often hidden and unwritten, patterns resist easy detection. You need a powerful magnifying glass to see them. Visible or not, they exert tremendous power in the workplace, guiding the behavior of veteran employees and capturing new ones the minute they walk in the door. They function like software programs that instruct the computer what to do. And like software, they can run smoothly or they can become infested with bugs and worms and malware.

2. **Collective:** People can come and go from your business, but the patterns tend to remain the same. They sit at the collective or systemic level in the organization. They are the agreements or the ways of relating between the parts of the organization. They might include, for example, the agreement that "we don't like to give bad news" or "we step down and micromanage," or "it's OK to bully and harass people around here." Think of a spiderweb as an analogy. Many threads (behaviors) weave together to form an overall web (pattern). Its collective nature means you can often see the same

pattern showing up in different parts of the organization. During my many years working in the trenches of culture change, I have seen too many leaders concentrate on the threads (the behaviors) instead of the patterns (the web) that govern behavior in the organization.

3. **Cocreated:** Patterns function like the rules of a dance, telling people how to move. "Put your left foot in, take your left foot out." Systems experts say that patterns are cocreated, meaning that it takes two to tango. To discover the key to changing a culture with minimum angst and disruption, you need to distinguish the dancers from the dance, the patterns from the behaviors.

Patterns can help the change. They can also ruin it. Productive and constructive ones provide a positive force that propels the organization to success. Creativity abounds. Honest and open communication stimulates creative collaboration; collaboration creates trust; trust binds people together; and care for one another stimulates respect for the needs of customers.

In sharp contrast, destructive patterns create a toxic environment in which people ultimately fail to deliver results. Self-interest prevails. Exclusion fosters alienation; secretiveness breeds mistrust; mistrust engenders defensiveness; and an unwillingness to accept accountability for mistakes leads to blaming others when something goes wrong. No one worries about providing excellent service to customers.

Constructive patterns inoculate employees against the ailments that can afflict and destroy an organization. Destructive ones infect new employees the minute they walk in the door. Both become deeply embedded in the culture, whether they arose in the organization's early days or have gradually developed over time. When you decide to change the culture, you can depend on constructive patterns to help the cause. Destructive ones can thwart your efforts every step of the way.

Patterns come in all shapes and sizes. Some you recognize right off the bat. Others retain their secrets and can take you by surprise when you uncover them. I remember the first time I visited "Solutions, Inc.," an international consulting firm, where I was attending a training course. As "Olga," a senior partner in the firm, escorted me through the offices, I noticed something rather unusual. Whenever someone met a colleague in the hallway, the two embraced with clear delight. It happened everywhere: in hallways, in conference rooms, in the cafeteria lines, even at the photocopier.

Later that morning, I ran into "Maxwell," a former colleague I had always found quite aloof and standoffish. He ran up and hugged me! I wondered if his body had been taken over by alien invaders. I could think of no better explanation for this surprising behavior. Later, Olga shed some light on the mystery. "Our CEO, 'Michael Williams,' believes that a company like ours needs to provide an example of compassion and human warmth. All this hugging is our way of showing one another and the world that we care about each other. It may seem strange at first, Siobhan, but it's such an ingrained habit we do it without even thinking about it."

In this era of hypersensitivity about violating personal space in ways that may be interpreted as harassment, most workplaces strongly discourage physical contact between employees. So, why did it seem not only acceptable, but even preferable, to hug one another at Solutions, Inc.? You can probably guess the answer: a deeply embedded pattern (Figure 2.4).

The idea of a warmer and more compassionate workplace had become an unwritten rule that signaled to employees that they could and should

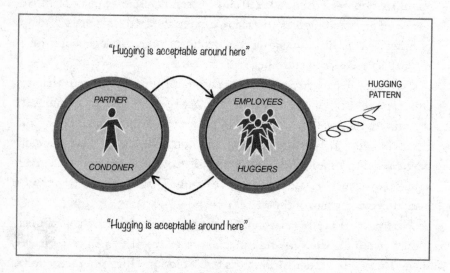

Figure 2.4. The Hugging Pattern

engage in a behavior many organizational leaders would deem unacceptable. It was a highly constructive behavior that fueled productivity at Solutions, Inc.

Think of patterns as the ways people relate to each other and the (often unwritten) rules of engagement. They are the agreements between the parts and the cocreated dynamics. You must typically look below the surface in order to discover them. People may come and go from your workplace, but the patterns tend to remain the same.

Deeply embedded patterns lie at the heart of workplace culture. Nothing will change until you identify and deal with those patterns.

*Patterns, not explicit values and behavior, govern culture.*

In Jonathan Cohen's case, he took this lesson to heart and used it to drive some major changes in the way his people thought about and pitched proposals to potential clients. A few months later, he called me to say: "Siobhan, I owe you another lunch. We just won a contract with the biggest new client AAA has landed in three years."

Having spent many years studying and teaching the subject, I found that it takes time for most leaders to learn how to spot the patterns in their organizations. A paradox lies at the heart of the problem. On the one hand, patterns resist easy detection; on the other hand, they follow certain basic rules. Once you understand those rules, you can become a master at pattern detection.

## LEARNING TO SEE PATTERNS

You can find patterns everywhere: in nature, in families, in nations. They develop according to certain rules. Understanding the rules that govern them will help you grasp the way they work in organizations.

Everything in nature follows a pattern you can see if you look closely enough. And once you see a pattern, you can figure out why and how it exists.

The six-sided symmetry of a snowflake, the chambered spiral shell of a mollusk, or the scattering of stars in the Milky Way all follow certain rules of mathematics, physics, chemistry, and biology.

Sorry to delve into a little science here, but this example shows how a keen observer can find simple explanations for complex phenomena like organizational culture. In 1917, the Scottish mathematical biologist D'Arcy Wentworth Thompson demonstrated that simple equations could describe the complex spiral patterns of animal horns and mollusk shells. These incredibly intricate and beautiful structures adhered to Fibonacci, or "golden spiral," ratios that generate a spiral where every quarter turn lies farther from the origin by a set factor. This holds true for the leaves of ferns, the trunks of trees, river systems, mountain ranges, clouds, coastlines, lightning strikes, and blood vessels.

Get ready for a little more science. Edward Lorenz, the American mathematician, meteorologist, and father of chaos theory, proposed what he called the "butterfly effect." This theory holds that something as small and seemingly insignificant as a butterfly flapping its wings in Brazil could set off a series of chain reactions that could eventually produce a tornado in Texas. Such seemingly random events, Lorenz claimed, actually follow a set of distinct and predictable rules (Figure 2.5).

In the human world, psychotherapists who study families have also examined the effects of patterns. Both positive and negative patterns tend to pass from generation to generation. Happy, well-adjusted families infused with love and respect and trust could produce generations of families displaying those same traits. The same effect occurs with unhappy families. Kids from violent homes could inherit a pattern of abuse, and those brought up in alcoholic households could end up with drinking problems.

This insight led psychotherapists working with dysfunctional families to treat the whole family system rather than just focus on the person who displayed the bad behavior. Physical and emotional abuse, for example, was a symptom of a deeper problem. To solve that problem, you need to discover the underlying pattern that drove and contributed to the behavior. What pattern governed the abuse? What caused the abuser to behave this way? What were the roles and rules of relating in the family? What roles did other family members play in co-creating the drama?

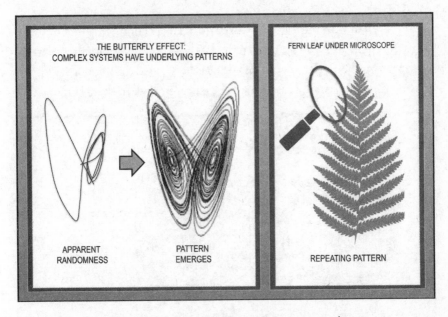

Figure 2.5. Patterns in Nature Demonstrate the
Order in Seemingly Chaotic Systems

Here is a case study about two work colleagues that illustrates how patterns emerge. "Luke Williams" and "Sean Taylor" are executives in a multinational software consulting company. Luke is a sales manager responsible for selling products and Sean is the relationship manager for clients in the energy sector. They are working on a big deal with a potential client, "GasNetworx" but they have an ongoing disagreement about who "owns" the client:

**Sean (relationship manager):** Why didn't you include me in the upcoming meeting with GasNetworx?

**Luke (sales manager):** It's a lunch, Sean, nothing formal.

**Sean:** I think I need to be involved in all meetings at this stage of the deal.

**Luke:** It's pretty casual. I'm just building the relationship.

**Sean:** Yes, and I'm the Relationship Manager on the deal, Luke.

**Luke:** Don't worry about it. I'll bring you in when I think it's necessary.

Rather than working together Luke and Sean are competing—about who owns the client and who gets the credit for the deal. This competitive pattern is impacting their relationship, as well as the service they are providing to clients. You could draw a diagram of the pattern between them (Figure 2.6).

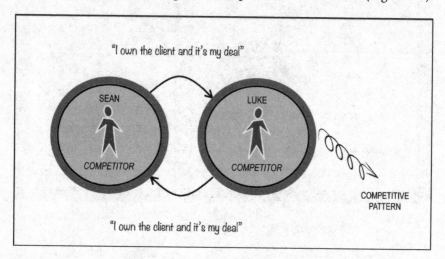

Figure 2.6. The Competitive Pattern

Whose fault is the ongoing conflict between Sean and Luke? As the diagram shows, each participant has stepped into the role of "competitor" to fuel the pattern. So, how do you break this negative competitive pattern? One of the colleagues needs to change his role from "competitor" to "collaborator." Sean starts by walking into Luke's office later that week:

**Sean (relationship manager):** How can I help with the GasNetworx deal?
**Luke (sales manager):** We are struggling a bit with the proposal.
**Sean:** What's the issue?
**Luke:** My sales team members have different views about what the client needs.
**Sean:** I know exactly what GasNetworx is looking for. I can share the intel from my interviews with you.
**Luke:** Great! We have more of a chance of landing the deal if we work together.
**Sean:** I agree!

That was the beginning of a shift in the pattern between Luke and Sean. You can apply this approach to any organizational pattern.

Cultural adjustments do not always come easily, speaking from my personal experience. I grew up in Ireland. As a child, I sang Celtic songs, ate Irish stew, and listened raptly to tales of goddesses, ancient kings, faeries, leprechauns, and the "other world." I could play the haunting "Lonesome Boatman" on a tin whistle and dance an Irish jig to entertain guests in our family home. My parents had done the same as kids, and so had their parents and grandparents. It was "how things work around here."

After I left Ireland, I spent time in England and the United States before settling down in Australia. What a different world I encountered there, a place drastically different from the rainy skies and green rolling hills of the Emerald Isle. I saw Australia as a yellow, sun burnt land, with endless blue skies and animals Noah forgot to take on the ark. The kangaroo! The koala! The wombat!

And don't get me started on the language. In the office my co-workers asked "What footie team do you barrack for?" I figured out pretty quickly that this meant that I was expected to find an Australian Rules football team to support. At work everyone seemed to be called a variation of their given name—Julia became Jules, Daniel became Danno, Brooke became Brookie, and my colleagues even tried to shorten my name to Shivy! It took me a while to adjust from my role as an Irish national to an Aussie. Like any pattern it was both simple and complex. Complicated because assimilating into a new environment required me to adjust to different ways—from the happy-go-lucky, positive, hardworking, and sport-loving nature of many of the people to the way that they talked. Simple once I saw the unwritten rules and redefined my role.

## RECOGNIZING THE INFLUENCE
## OF SOCIETAL PATTERNS

Societal patterns can strongly influence organizational patterns. If you're dealing with patterns held collectively in a societal or national culture, then the job of changing an organization's culture just got a whole lot tougher. "Myra Patel," the head of diversity at "ToughGlass, Ltd." (TGL), a European glass-manufacturing company headquartered in England, discovered this the hard way. Myra and I met at a change management conference in Stockholm, where we discussed her culture challenge over coffee. She told me an interesting story: "We've got a target of 35 percent females employed at TGL, which, when you think about it, is really not that ambitious. But we've been stuck at 30 percent for the last two years. I've tried everything, Siobhan, but I don't know how to move the dial on these diversity stats. Any ideas?"

"What have you done so far?" I inquired.

Myra took a quick breath. "We've developed a compelling business case for why diversity matters, we've invested in putting more than two hundred leaders through an intensive two-day diversity and inclusion training program, and we've implemented a best practice mentoring program to help women take charge of their careers. But nothing has changed. Here, look."

Myra pulled her iPad out of her handbag and popped open reports full of detailed company statistics and quantitative data. As I scanned the numbers, I noted that women filled 70 percent of TGL's support staff roles, while men performed 70 percent of the more senior leadership roles (from the CEO to front-line managers). I looked up at Myra. "You can talk about diversity until the cows come home, but if you don't add more women to your leadership roles, even if you hit your 35 percent target, those added women will be working in support and administration. I've got one suggestion. You need to uncover the underlying issues and the patterns that drive behavior in your company."

I went on to explain that Myra seemed to be addressing symptoms, rather than the underlying pattern. To reach the diversity target, the executives at TGL needed to see the unwritten rule that had created the current gender gap. "You've done a good job at one level," I said. "However, it seems that you've been addressing the behaviors rather than patterns. Yes, you've accomplished a lot by building women's confidence, coaching young females to take charge of their careers, and helping leaders identify unconscious biases, but you have not tackled the deeply embedded TGL pattern that places men in leadership roles and women in support roles. This implicit, unwritten rule has kept your dial at 30 percent."

Myra's struggles did not surprise me, because the particular pattern she wanted to change affects not only individual organizations, but society as a whole. To progress toward her 35 percent goal, she needed to wrestle with a societal problem that guided gender attitudes at a national level. You can trace the unwritten rules that confer power on men and place women in subservient roles to the dawn of the human race. Asking any HR manager to change that history is a tall order indeed. You know me; I like to draw diagrams (Figure 2.7).

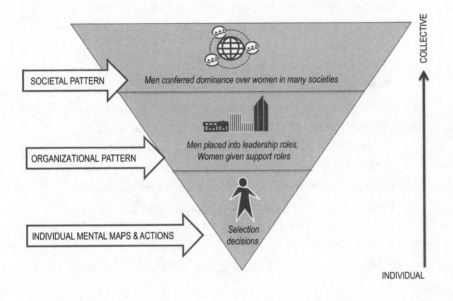

Figure 2.7. Patterns Sit at the Collective Level

When it comes to putting more women in leadership roles, most companies in most countries must climb a very steep hill. While the patterns infuse a given organization with long-standing ideas about the supportive role of women in the workplace, centuries of human and national patterns dictate that women fulfill those same roles in society. That's a deeply embedded pattern to break and often-unconscious beliefs to conquer before companies achieve greater gender balance in positions of power.

During culture change successful leaders look for the big patterns that drive the culture. Only when you grasp the cocreated nature of the big patterns that are running your business and the connections between the parts (that are fueling these patterns) can you feel confident about changing the culture.

## · POINTS TO REMEMBER ·

- Culture definition: The patterns or agreements that determine how the business operates or, simply, how things work around here.
- The three key elements of culture are the *Mental Maps*, *Roles*, and *Patterns*.
- *Mental Maps* are images, points of view, and perceptions that people hold that help them navigate the world.
- *Roles* dictate behavior, just as much as personality.
- *Patterns* are the ways of relating or agreements between the parts, that determine how the business operates.
- Patterns lie at the heart of workplace culture.

# 3

# PREPARE
# FOR CHANGE

## Diagnosing Your Current
## Business Environment

Now that you understand the basics of workplace culture, *Mental Maps*, *Roles*, and *Patterns*, you can think about embarking on your own change journey. Embarking on culture change is similar, in some ways, to setting sail on a sea voyage. As the leader, you must know your destination, chart your path, make necessary course corrections, and constantly diagnose the full business environment before, during, and after the journey.

Imagine setting sail for unexplored and possibly dangerous regions, which ancient mapmakers flagged with the cautionary words: "There be dragons." Other organizations may have traveled into similar uncharted territory, but your own organization will be making its own unique journey. When leaders talk about their culture change, they often describe it as a rather logical, step-by-step process. They knew where they wanted to go, perhaps to a culture imbued with agility and innovation; they had charted a clear course to get there, they went from point A, to point B, to point C, and then they reached their destination relatively unscathed. That sounds pretty straightforward. But, in fact, no culture change initiative ever follows a straight line.

In an unpredictable, disruptive, and fast-changing business environment, perennially successful companies constantly reinvent themselves and their culture. The Italian papermaking company Fabriano offers a case in point. Several years ago, while I was vacationing in Venice, Italy, I found a beautiful handcrafted notebook that would make a perfect gift for a cat-sitting friend back home. In a conversation with the shopkeeper, I discovered that the notebook had been manufactured in Fabriano's mills in the Marche region, where the company has been making paper since the 1200s. Amazingly, Fabriano has thrived for more than 750 years, weathering the Middle Ages, the Industrial Revolution, World Wars I and II, and the age of digital technology.

How had Fabriano remained agile and reinvented itself throughout the ages? In the Middle Ages, the firm invented the watermark, which enabled it to make money notes for European central banks. During the Industrial Revolution, it introduced more efficient papermaking processes that allowed the company to compete globally. Fabriano continued to innovate by using hydroelectricity to generate power and today produces even more electricity than it needs for its operations. It may sound straight-forward, in retrospect. But if you look into the company's history, you will see that it followed a circuitous path, with many detours and surprising twists and turns along the way (Figure 3.1).

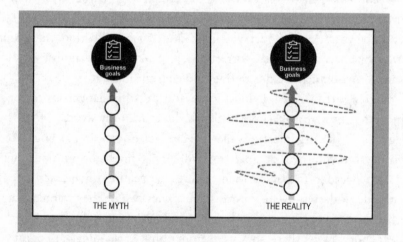

Figure 3.1. Culture Change Does Not Follow a Straight Path

Given the complexities of workplace culture, you must be fully prepared before you embark on this type of change. Before you move to action, I recommend that you carry out a comprehensive assessment of what's going on in the broader business environment, as well as in the workplace.

## SCANNING THE MARKETPLACE

You may recall The Culture Disruptor, with the four steps for successful culture change. Each subsequent chapter in this book relates to one of these four steps, and you can tell which step it covers by the icon at the start of the chapter: *Diagnose* (stethoscope), *Reframe* the roles (pair of glasses), *Break* the pattern (broken chain), and *Consolidate* the gains (upward spiral). This chapter deals with the first step on The Culture Disruptor, which is to Diagnose what's going in the external environment, before you move to action (Figure 3.2).

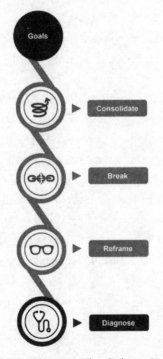

Figure 3.2. The First Step on The Culture Disruptor: Diagnose

The most successful change leaders carefully examine both the internal and the external environment to determine exactly what's going on inside their own organization (the subject of the next chapter) and in the marketplace. Externally, they zoom in on current trends and developments just beginning to appear on the distant horizon. The future may resist accurate prediction, but you can always detect little clues to the internal changes you must make in order to thrive long term. Take Netflix, for example. Netflix cofounder and CEO Reed Hastings launched the enterprise as a brick-and-mortar chain of retail video-rental stores that offered a convenient way for customers to view movies in their own homes. Looking to the horizon, however, Hastings changed his business model when he saw an even more convenient way to deliver movies by mailing them to viewers. This move made their stores obsolete and put rival Blockbuster out of business. Ever vigilant, Netflix once again changed its own business when Hastings looked ahead to a digital future and began providing movies and television shows online.

Many executives would feel quite content with this string of innovations. Not Hastings. In 2011, Netflix went from content provider to content maker when it put together the hit series *House of Cards*. It was an incredibly bold and risky move, taking on the century-old television and movie production system in Hollywood and New York, but the gamble paid off at the 2018 Emmy awards. Netflix was nominated for more awards than any other entertainment firm: 112 for its forty Emmy-nominated series. The company that had put Blockbuster out of business had chosen to battle toe-to-toe with once dominant HBO, and it was winning the fight. According to *Variety*, by the end of 2018, the company had exploded its market to 137 million subscribers around the world, and it had plans to spend more than $15 billion on content in 2019.

Reed Hastings had put his finger on the pulse of an industry and had detected symptoms of revolutionary change more astutely than his competitors. GE's Jack Welch, Apple's Steve Jobs, and Amazon's Jeff Bezos also saw a future others did not. I like that old phrase "captains of industry," because it suggests a leader standing on the bridge of the ship, constantly scanning the horizon for threats ahead and quicker routes to the future. At great companies, captain after captain does the same.

American Express started out as a shipping company. A new CEO looked ahead, saw a new need, and began selling money orders and traveler's checks.

The next CEO of AMEX, Frederick Small, took the company into the travel agency business and disrupted freight forwarding. Following in his footsteps, Ralph Reed, the next AMEX CEO, created the American Express charge card, thereby disrupting the traveler's check business. In recent years, the company evolved into a conglomerate, buying insurance companies and moving into financial services. By constantly diagnosing the business environment, AMEX's leaders could see when they needed to steer the organization in a new direction.

The business world is filled with examples of company downfalls, brought about by a failure to notice and respond (appropriately) to what was going on in the external environment. Remember Blockbuster? And don't forget Eastman Kodak (sunk by digital photography), Sears and Toys "R" Us (wrecked by online retailers), and Yahoo (smashed by Google). You can't blame it all on an individual leader, but you can blame it on a culture that was not capable of adapting rapidly enough to the challenges in the marketplace.

## SEEING THE THREATS ON THE HORIZON

Successful leaders remain ever vigilant for potential opportunities and threats on the horizon. The threats can emerge slowly over time and be so subtle that they are hard to detect. Other shifts can happen rapidly and have a dramatic impact on the financial health of the organization. Although I use the word threats, often these challenges can be opportunities for the company to grow and evolve. Leaders can never become complacent to these shifts in marketplace dynamics. Contrary to the old saying, complacency has killed more cats than curiosity ever did. Perhaps you remember this bit of dialogue from Ernest Hemingway's *The Sun Also Rises*:

"How did you go bankrupt?"
"Two ways. Gradually, then suddenly."

Nokia, the Finnish firm that served as the poster child for innovative technology in the late 1990s, led the mobile phone revolution. The name represented one of the most respected and valuable brands globally. However, in 2007, its dominance began to fade until, a mere shadow of its former self, Microsoft bought it in 2013.

How did this giant fall so rapidly? It paid too little attention to Apple and the iPhone, a rival product that would become almost synonymous with the word "smartphone." Was it a failure to keep an eye on developing technology? Yes and no. Yes, Apple innovated the product into a handheld computer, but it was Nokia's complacent culture that precipitated its downfall. In the 1990s, the Finnish company had developed a prototype touchscreen phone (before Apple launched the iPhone) that could have wiped out every competitor at the time.

Despite a long history of adaptive innovation, a culture of complacency had emerged at Nokia. Having achieved such wild success on the world stage, Nokia's executives enjoyed rock-star status in Finland. They appeared to hold a dangerous assumption that Nokia's products were unbeatable and admiring their past successes, rather than emerging players in the marketplace, they did not see the twin threats of Apple and Android bearing down on them.

Even worse, the executives at Nokia failed to sustain their once innovative culture, focusing more on selling and servicing existing products than on creating new leading-edge offerings. The evolving culture did not emphasize collaboration. Software engineers, who could have made Nokia's phones more user friendly, took a back seat to the hardware engineers, who designed and built the phones. At Apple, on the other hand, the hardware and software engineers worked together to create apps that delighted its customers.

Cultures composed of people who bring diverse backgrounds and talents to the enterprise come up with more creative solutions—better than those who hire and promote people who think and behave the same way. In Nokia's case, the company drew its senior executives from its native Finland. This fostered a cookie-cutter culture where people looked alike, thought alike, and behaved alike. This led to a sort of groupthink that made it hard to look beyond the near horizon to see changes sweeping into the marketplace. By the time Nokia's leaders saw the impending dangers, the company was already in trouble.

Over the course of my career, I have witnessed this phenomenon several times. For example, "BuildItPro," an underperforming global infrastructure company managing projects across America and Europe, had expanded rapidly. Despite that growth, it had faltered, and the company found itself mired in deep financial trouble. When "Ben Harkness," the newly appointed CEO, walked into the job he knew he needed to gain a firm grasp on the situation before making any bold moves to get the company back on track. As he explained to me, "Competition is heating up, with new players entering the marketplace, yet everyone at BuildItPro seems to be lulled into this false sense of security that we can keep doing things the way we've always done them."

I asked Ben a follow-up question: "What, exactly, must you change?"

Ben did not skip a beat. "Clients are moving away from cost-reimbursable, or 'soft,' contracts where they paid us an agreed-upon margin on top of the project costs. Now they demand inflexible, fixed-price, or 'hard' contracts. This is forcing us to rethink our old approach to financial management. Sixty percent of our projects are running in the red."

If BuildItPro didn't start managing its costs much more effectively, it would continue hemorrhaging profits. A tour of the company's major projects revealed a common mistake. Project managers were doing a lot of favors for clients in order to keep them happy, but they were not charging for these so-called favors. For example, if an engineer discovered a leaky pipe or a faulty machine, he would fix it at no charge to the customer. All this pro-bono work was costing the company dearly.

I saw the problem. "Your managers are behaving as if they are still operating in a 'soft contract' world, where the extra work gets charged to the client. They have defined their role as relationship-builders who must satisfy customers at all costs. You need to reframe their roles from 'relationship managers' to 'cost-conscious providers' and start charging for their work."

That simple suggestion enabled Ben to initiate a culture-change campaign. We'll look more closely at his change initiative later in this chapter, but for now I want you to take one lesson from Ben's story. Once he took a step back he could see that the business environment had changed but that the culture at BuildItPro had remained the same. Ben knew that he would need to rapidly adjust or face the prospect that the company would go into further decline.

•    •    •

## GOING BEYOND GOOD

In today's fiercely competitive business environment, good is never good enough. Only excellence will prevail. But how do you determine what excellence means in your industry? Is it the financial result announced by your rivals? Well, the numbers provide a yardstick for measuring success, but yardsticks do not create disruptive value that will allow you to break away from your competitors. Cultures do. To figure out where you stand in relationship to everyone else in your competitive world, you need to look at the cultures that drive their success. "Widget, Inc.," sells more widgets and makes more profit, but *how* does it do that? It has created a culture that gets those results.

When ANZ bank's John McFarlane recognized the need to transform his company's toxic culture, he started by examining what excellence looked like in top companies. He sent one of his senior executives, Chelvi Satyendra, on a global study tour to visit companies with exceptional service cultures around the globe. Chelvi looked beyond the banking sector for answers, visiting technology, retail, and professional service companies renowned for exceptional customer service. When he brought back the findings to ANZ's leadership team, Chelvi offered one strong conclusion: The best in class in every industry invested heavily in building strong personal relationships with customers. Relationship building was at the core of these cultures. Managers talked to clients regularly, detected grievances early, and resolved issues immediately. This feedback may seem rather obvious, but it opened a lot of eyes at ANZ. Many of its managers sat in the head office all day and rarely spoke to customers. John and his leadership team now knew they would need to shift this pattern, if they were to transform the culture at ANZ into one that compared with the best globally.

Like John McFarlane, successful change leaders take a regular step back to examine what's emerging in the marketplace. They gather intelligence from numerous sources about what's going on locally and in other parts of the world. They may keep an eye on the latest benchmarking data, network broadly inside and outside the industry, or ask an independent consultant for an unvarnished view of how the company is faring. However they do it, these leaders are never complacent about keeping a constant check on market conditions.

By the way, the leader does not have to scan the horizon alone. She can invite others to join her there and ask them to share what they see emerging in the future. John McFarlane did just that to regain the community's trust in the bank's operations. The data told him that the bank had the lowest customer satisfaction ratings amongst the big banks, and he sought to transform it into a company that truly cared about its customers' needs. Since John knew he could not solve this problem on his own, he decided to engage the bank's thirty-two thousand employees in finding the best solutions. As a key step, he invited staff to participate in structured interviews designed to explore the bank's purpose in society. When my team issued a call for people who might like to discuss this question, we expected a trickle of interest. Within a week, however, more than one thousand employees from across the organization had volunteered to participate in the interview program. It was a rather simple process. We paired each volunteer with a colleague and showed the pair how to use a fast-forward technique (based on David Coop-errider's Appreciative Inquiry approach) by asking a specific question:

*Imagine that you walk into ANZ in three years' time and everything is working as it should be. All the issues have been resolved. Describe what you see happening at this time. What is the bank's purpose in society? How did this change come about?*

The fast-forward technique invited employees to gaze into the future, im-agining the results of their hopes and dreams for a better bank that fulfills a vital purpose in society. We aimed for a rich mix of participants. Executives sat down with bank tellers to discuss the topic over coffee. IT professionals explored possibilities with risk analysts. Seasoned institutional bankers shared ideas with recent recruits. Employees from all over ANZ began to put their dreams into words as they delved deeply into just what sort of organi-zation they imagined in the future, one that would delight customers, share-holders, employees, and the broader community.

Mental maps began to change as more and more people turned away from the current inward-looking culture and began to imagine one that looked outward to see and fulfill customer and societal needs. ANZ's people did not want to behave like cold, unemotional robots; they wanted to play the more satisfying role of human beings concerned with the welfare of others. More and more people found the words to describe the idea of a more human organization. Now we needed to translate those words into action. After we collected and compiled the findings of the interview program, we shared the results widely throughout the organization. We even asked an artist to create concrete images that showed ANZ's people fulfilling the new vision. Soon these drawings appeared on the walls of meeting rooms, reminding people of the new culture ANZ wanted to create.

Questions. Ideas. Words. Actions. It did not happen overnight, of course, but gradually ANZ's leaders began to hear and share stories of the new culture in action. Employees were going out of their way to help one another, their customers, and the communities they served. If a teller was wrestling with a difficult customer problem, colleagues eagerly jumped to his aid. If a customer made an unusual request for service, a manager did the best she could to satisfy it. Individuals and teams went beyond the traditional boundaries of their role to give back to their local communities by, for instance, building houses for the homeless or teaching money management skills to the most vulnerable members of the community.

Take one lesson from ANZ's transformation. When you are standing in the middle of a significant business challenge, it's often hard to see a solution. John McFarlane cast his eyes to the future and asked his people to do the same. Unwilling to be just a good bank, he urged his people to help him make it an excellent one. Rather than focusing on what was wrong with ANZ, he urged people to imagine what they could do to make it better. This begs one crucial question: *Why should you make such a dramatic and possibly wrenching change?*

## ACCURATELY ASSESSING
## YOUR BUSINESS NEEDS

There are good companies and bad companies, good cultures and bad cultures, good workplaces and bad workplaces, but one rule always applies: Every company, every culture, and every workplace must deliver the business results an organization needs in order to keep its workforce employed, its customers delighted, and its community well served. You don't change your culture for the sake of change, you change it to meet your business needs. That may seem excruciatingly obvious, but leaders can fail to make that connection.

Consider the experiences of two very different organizations: "Timbuktu Global" and the "3rd Infantry Division." Both have taken their key leaders to an off-site retreat for their annual conference. The Timbuktu Global team members spend every minute discussing how they can best exploit emerging market trends to achieve their business goals. They resolve to develop world-class products that will stay ahead of what their competitors offer. Research and development (R&D), supply chain, marketing, sales, and HR leaders on the team strive to come up with the most leading-edge ideas to achieve excellence in the industry. As the retreat draws to a close, the CEO concludes that in order to achieve these goals, "We need an innovative culture that inspires our people to come up with ideas that dazzle our clients!"

The members of the other team, the top brass of the 3rd Infantry Division, spend their retreat discussing the current state of military affairs. Unconventional enemy tactics, such as the use of IEDs and bomb-laden cars and trucks, have changed the landscape of battle. "In this changed environment, how can we minimize both military and civilian deaths?" The general closes the session with stirring words: "Discipline! We need ironclad strategies to build the most disciplined military culture on Earth."

Now, which retreat worked best? Timbuktu Global did what it needed to do in its world. And the 3rd Infantry Division did what it needed to do in its world. Both retreats succeeded, because they addressed what each culture needed to do to achieve desired results. Smart culture-builders define their business needs before they take step one.

Let's return to the BuildItPro case we discussed earlier in this chapter. You will recall that Ben Harkness had called me for help when he decided he needed to make a major culture change in his organization. We pinpointed the central issue: the need for the company's managers to move from relationship managers to cost-conscious providers. Once Ben grasped that idea, he set the change wheels in motion. After a few months, he called me again. I hoped to hear good news, but instead I listened as Ben fumed over the phone: "It's driving me nuts! We're going around in circles! No matter what I try, people keep falling back into their old habits. I can't figure it out."

To get to the bottom of this mystery, I agreed to meet with Ben's leadership team. I suspected that the problem stemmed from the lack of a clear understanding about exactly where Ben wanted the culture change to take the company. I opened the meeting with a question that raised a few eyebrows. I drew a diagram (Figure 3.3) on the whiteboard then asked, "What business is BuildItPro in?"

"Kaili Waliki," the oil and gas sector leader smiled. "Well, that's totally obvious. We are in the business of supplying clients with the resources they need to design, construct, and maintain their physical assets."

"Ahmed Rashad," the head of strategy, frowned. "No, no, no, Kaili! That is not true. At the recent board meeting, we described our mission clearly. We are a consulting firm that provides clients with innovative solutions to build and maintain their physical assets." Other team members offered their own opinions. It soon grew painfully apparent that no two executives framed BuildItPro's mission exactly the same way, though they fell into either the

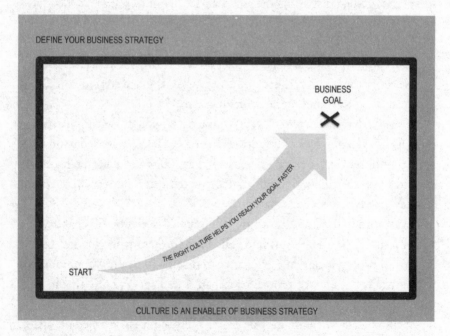

Figure 3.3. Begin with the End in Mind

Kaili or Ahmed camp. I asked another question. "Are you fish or fowl, a re-source provider or a consulting outfit, or something else entirely?"

The group looked puzzled. Ben offered his own opinion. "Aren't they much the same?"

"On the surface, perhaps. But think about it. A resource provider would need to supply the right people to do the job in a timely and efficient manner. A consulting firm would need to look for creative ways to get the job done. It's all about your business need. What do you *need* to do to accomplish your goals?"

Ben got it. "We've been spinning around in circles because we lacked a clear understanding of who we are, what we do, and where we want to go."

Spot on! The team members had begun the change journey without a clear destination in mind. Without this agreement on the business goals, they had changed their minds about the culture they required. The end re-sult was that they had shifted from one culture plan to the next and made little progress. It was clear that the leadership team needed to get alignment on the BuildItPro business purpose and goals before proceeding. We spent the rest of the afternoon exploring the fundamental question: "What busi-ness are we in?" Could we craft a clear, concise, and compelling strategy statement that everyone understood and could strive to achieve? It took a few hours to reach a consensus, which Ben wrote on the whiteboard:

"We provide creative and cost-effective solutions for building, maintain-ing, and operating physical assets."

Team members might refine this statement, but for now it gave them what they needed to begin designing a culture that would effectively implement the strategy. As you saw earlier in the chapter, BuildItPro needed to shift from the role of relationship managers to cost-conscious providers. That's why the new strategy statement included the term "cost-effective." The state-ment included the word "creative" for two reasons. One: BuildItPro needed to impress potential clients with its innovative approaches. Two: It would take a different way of working to maintain positive relationship with clients *and* charge them for all those extra little favors.

No matter how far your culture change initiative may take you, it always begins with one surefooted first step. And that first step must be in the right direction: toward your ultimate business goals.

## DECIDING HOW YOU
## WILL MEASURE PROGRESS

Leaders who set a change initiative in motion and expect it to move forward without a hitch can, like Ben Harkness, end up wondering why progress has slowed to a crawl or halted altogether. As with any long journey, you need to set a series of milestones or benchmarks that tell you where you stand along the path to your final destination. Determining the metrics at the start of the change journey, allows you to track your progress in changing your business from the current to the desired culture.

*You can't change what you can't measure.*

Whatever measuring process you use, you need to apply it to the right variables. If you want to build a first-rate customer service culture, you might do what Tony Hsieh, CEO of Zappos (the online shoe and clothing retailer), did to measure satisfied customers. Zappos achieved tremendous customer loyalty by pursuing Hsieh's goal to "knock their shoes off" with great service. He believed that his company should do whatever it took to keep customers happy, because he held the view that even a seemingly costly gesture will, in the long run, result in profits. He applies the same philosophy to employees and vendors.

In his book *Delivering Happiness*, Hsieh describes the measurements he uses to make sure Zappos' culture delivers a memorable customer experience. For example, he insisted that the company's call center staff strive to make an emotional connection with customers. Building a relationship at that level takes more time than the usual "May I help you?" service interaction, but it pays off. Returning customers account for 75 percent of Zappos sales. Customers who desire service over speed like doing business with Zappos because the call center staff treats them more like friends than sales targets. While typical call center managers measure performance in terms of "average time per call," Zappos uses a different metric that tells management how many customers keep coming back to buy shoes. Who says you can't measure happiness? Not Tony Hsieh. As he writes in his book, "We're not trying to maximize efficiency. We're trying to maximize the customer experience."

"Happiness experience" measurements come into play every day at Zappos. How many "Wow!" moments are we creating for our customers? How many customers feel that we really care about them? How many times has this customer come back to buy another pair of shoes? Measurements like these tell the company's leaders how much progress they have made toward their ambition to create a customer-centric workplace culture.

How will you measure progress toward *your* culture goal? If you provide service in the banking sector, you might do what ANZ's John McFarlane did. Hoping to build a best-in-class service culture not unlike Zappos, McFarlane relied on external benchmarks to measure exactly where the bank stood at the beginning of the change journey. To diagnose the bank's environment at that time (2000), he used Richard Barrett's Cultural Transformation Tools (CTT) *Values Assessment Survey* and McKinsey's *Performance Ethic Survey*. The *Values Assessment Survey* invited employees to select ten values that best described the current culture at ANZ. The top three were:

- Cost reduction
- Profit
- Shareholder value

Other values selected by employees included such words and phrases as "bureaucratic," "hierarchical," "long hours," and "risk aversion." I had seldom seen results this bad, with so many limiting values. Companies with this type of profile have enormous amounts of *entropy*, which means that value is leaking from the organization on a daily basis. This assessment rang a loud alarm bell: it confirmed that employees saw ANZ as a company that was focused almost exclusively on the needs of shareholders and that could not care less about their welfare or customer needs.

In relation to employee welfare, McFarlane also benchmarked staff satisfaction against other companies. Compared to highly engaged cultures where the vast majority of workers expressed great satisfaction with the way their employer treated them, less than half of ANZ's people liked working at the bank. Of the thirty-two thousand employees, 49 percent felt so disengaged that they would gladly work at anything but their present jobs.

McKinsey's *Performance Ethic Survey* benchmarking exercise compared ANZ's culture to other high-performing companies. While the results reinforced ANZ's strengths in financial and operational areas, it revealed that the bank ranked below average in terms of how employees worked together to get the job done and in defining a clear and compelling mission. As I weighed these findings, I concluded that human relationships had broken down to the point where many people did not feel the least bit inspired to get great results for the organization.

When McFarlane asked an outside consulting firm to measure customer satisfaction, he once again found disappointing results. When compared to other big banks, ANZ ranked last in this category. All the measurements painted a grim but accurate picture of the bank's current business environment. They told McFarlane and his executive team that the path to the future would be a long and dusty road indeed.

---

### · POINTS TO REMEMBER ·

- Culture change never follows a straight line.
- Successful change leaders diagnose the internal and external business environment.
- Scanning the environment can reveal key signals about how your business might need to adapt.
- An important starting point is to find out what excellence looks like.
- The culture must always align with the business needs.
- Metrics help you establish where you started, and your change progress.

# 4

# DIAGNOSE THE
# CURRENT CULTURE

## Looking for the
## Big Patterns

If you occasionally suffer crushing headaches and frequent bouts of fatigue, you might worry that you've come down with a serious ailment, perhaps an impending stroke. When I couldn't shake those symptoms, I went to see my doctor. After giving me a thorough checkup, she announced a surprising cure. "Siobhan, you might need glasses."

"Ah, that makes sense!" I thought. She went on to explain that folks my age can develop farsightedness (hyperopia) and that the strain of compensating for that problem can create exactly the symptoms I was experiencing. When an ophthalmologist confirmed my doctor's diagnosis, I found myself shopping for designer frames. I might be getting old, but at least I can see clearly now!

The health of a corporate culture requires the correct diagnosis, one that goes beyond symptoms and knee-jerk conclusions to the underlying causes of the problem. What, you must ask yourself, is creating the noise? You must carefully assess the situation. And, of course, a second opinion always helps.

When organizational leaders realize that they are dealing with a sick culture, they usually feel such enormous pressure to cure it that they make hasty decisions they soon regret. With the wrong medicine, the culture's health keeps declining until not even the most radical treatment can revive it. Over the years, I have seen a lot of quick-fix solutions create disastrous problems of their own. Suppose I had done something radical when I started getting those headaches. No amount of radiation treatment or chemotherapy would have corrected my vision, and I would have lost all my hair into the bargain.

In the first step on The Culture Disruptor, *Diagnose*, you explore and pinpoint what really ails you. How do you avoid jumping too quickly to solutions when facing a crisis? How do you identify the real issues that are holding your business back from achieving its full potential? Until you see and address the underlying causes, you will continue to experience the reoccurring noise in your workplace.

## LEARNING BY WALKING AROUND

Effective change leaders don't just sit on their perches high in the C-suite; they spend a lot of time walking around the organization, talking to people at every level in every functional area, and keenly observing "how things work around here." They bring a good set of eyes and ears to the task, observing the ways of relating and listening carefully to what people say about their work, their colleagues, their department, their boss, and the company. When I walked into ANZ's headquarters in 2001 for what would turn into a seven-year culture change project, I was overwhelmed by the opulence of the lobby. I peered up at giant marble pillars stretched high up to gothic ceilings. I examined the beautiful white leather sofas that looked as if no one ever sat in them, and I felt my feet sink into the plush, woolen carpet. On ANZ's mid-level floors, managers worked in bright, open-plan spaces with an abundance of natural light. The executive suites on the top level boasted expensive works of art and sweeping views of Melbourne.

A visit to the bank's branches later that week told a very different story. The décor reminded me of Ebenezer Scrooge's office in *A Christmas Carol*, cold and uninviting, with threadbare carpets, paint peeling from barren walls, and a ceiling dappled with water stains. Sad-looking customers stood in long lines, shifting from foot to foot as they waited for someone to help them. Meanwhile, the staff looked harried and haggard as they peered through the bulletproof glass that separated them from their customers. They seemed to repeat the same excuse to each customer, "I can't help you because that decision is made in the head office."

*Effective change leaders bring*
*keen eyes and ears to the work.*

My strolls around head office and the branches filled my head with important data about ANZ's current culture. The people in head office were far removed from the realities of working life in the branches and the needs of customers. Previous management had seen the branch network as an expense item or cost on the balance sheet. If the top execs viewed the branches as little more than costly overhead, why should the branch tellers treat customers any differently?

Publishing consultant "Brandon James" told me a personal story that reminds me of what I discovered by walking around ANZ's offices. Back in the seventies, Brandon was working as an editor at "Small and Heart," a highly profitable, medium-sized publisher of lifestyle books based in California. Then, out of the blue, the company's owners sold it to "Big Books," a huge global conglomerate. Small and Heart (S&H) had built a highly author-centric culture. Authors loved working with everyone at S&H. As Brandon described it: "S&H's functional departments worked in the same one-story office building. Editors loved and championed their authors, and their feeling of respect spread to the contract and accounting functions. Editorial committees made decisions in days, contracts popped out a day after we completed negotiations, and accounting seldom made a mistake, but when they did, they corrected it immediately."

After the merger, all that changed. Big Books' executives operated out of Toronto, and the contracts and accounting staff worked in New Jersey. Now it took two months to make a decision to publish a new book, two more months for a contract to come from New Jersey, and yet another two months to correct frequent accounting errors.

According to Brandon, "The folks in contracts and accounting saw authors as necessary evils. As far as the accounting department was concerned, authors were not the source of the income that paid everyone's salaries but greedy outsiders who soaked up advances and royalties under 'accounts payable.' To a contract administrator, putting together a new contract was a pain in the neck." During a series of conversations, Brandon asked people in all of the company's functional areas how they felt about the merger. Brandon listened carefully to the back-office people as they vented a lot of anger and frustration. Taking it all to heart, he soon quit to start his consulting company. Over the next several years, S&H lost many of its most talented editors and authors to competitors. The moral of this story: Brandon just needed to walk around S&H's offices to see and hear the clues to a dismal future.

In sharp contrast, I remember my first day walking around the headquarters of a company with a much happier culture. In 2016, I went to work as head of HR for DuluxGroup, the Australian-based paints and consumer goods company. I vividly recall the morning I arrived at the company headquarters for my job interview. The company's CEO, Patrick Houlihan, met me in the reception area and accompanied me to his office on the third floor. I had expected an assistant, not the boss, to usher me upstairs. This small gesture told me a lot about DuluxGroup's culture. It was a place where the big boss would roll up his sleeves and work arm in arm with his people to get results. And, boy, did Patrick and his people get results. In just eight years, DuluxGroup had almost quadrupled its market value from $850 million to more than $3 billion. Patrick Houlihan had worked for the company for more than thirty years, climbing the ladder from his first job as a junior chemist to his current position. He knew the company inside out. He could tell you when an employee had joined the firm and could recount stories about that person's career achievements over the years. Walk around DuluxGroup's offices, and you saw a vibrant, healthy culture in action.

Observant leaders look and listen for subtle clues to a culture's health. They know when tellers treat their customers with a dismissive attitude; they know when support staff sees authors as nuisances; they notice if a manager remembers the birthdays and employment anniversaries of every person on the team. As you walk around your business, try to see it with fresh eyes and listen with open ears. What you see and hear might surprise you.

## PRESSING THE PAUSE BUTTON

Impatience can kill a change initiative before it even gets started. As you try to figure out what's going on inside your business, you can often find yourself under considerable pressure to implement a quick solution. A chorus of voices may be demanding decisive action. You worry that a delay will cost you the support of your board, your boss, your customers, your employees, your suppliers, and the general public. I have found, however, that when everyone is shouting for a quick fix, you should find the courage to hit the pause button.

*If you move too swiftly to solve a problem,*
*you may only make it worse.*

"Waterworks," a water-system maintenance company that had just won a ten-year contract with the government agency, "Metro City," offers a good case in point. When "Chloe Khan" began her stint as the manager at Waterworks, she wanted to get off to a good start, but her feet had barely hit the ground before she got an angry call from her contact at Metro City, a no-nonsense man named "Fernando Garcia." Fernando did not mince words. "I'm worried about your team, Ms. Khan. I'm looking at some alarming performance stats, and I've got too many customers complaining about slow and shoddy repairs. You need to fix the problem, and fast!"

Chloe hung up the phone feeling a little desperate. She knew about Fernando's reputation for impatience with contractors. He had cancelled the contract with the firm that had preceded Waterworks. Now it seemed that Chloe might be looking for a new job before she even started in this one. Eager to satisfy Fernando's complaint, she called an urgent meeting with her management team. "We've got a big problem, people. Fernando over at Metro City is furious. What are we doing wrong?"

"Anika Petrov," the head of quality at Waterworks, didn't hold back. "Our supervisors are the problem. They do not know how to get their maintenance crews on board with our new work procedures. Maybe our supervisors just need some leadership training." Others around the table nodded their heads in agreement. Yes, the blame lay at the feet of the inept supervisors.

Chloe called me for some advice. The next day, I sat in her office, sharing a pot of tea. She got right to the point. "I need to build a leadership training program for my supervisors. Can you help?"

Of course I could, but I was not sure she was addressing the underlying cause of the problem. "Do you mind if we take a step back? Tell me a little bit about the team's history. What have you learned since you became their boss?"

Chloe rattled off a list of problems, from a reluctance to adopt new procedures to an unusual number of absences from work. "The whole team seems mired in the past and very, very slow to change anything. And it's not just the workers. The supervisors act as if they are entitled to do things their own way. Their way is the old way, and that is what has gotten us into this mess."

"Well, it seems you have more of a culture issue than a leadership problem," I mused. "How about we take time to perform a thorough culture assessment before you send the supervisors off to leadership school?"

Chloe hesitated before nodding agreement. "OK, but we've got to get moving. If I can't show big-time progress in three weeks, Fernando's going to review our contract."

By agreeing to press the pause button, Chloe avoided one of the biggest pitfalls in culture work: moving to action before you have fully understood the underlying issues. To find those underlying issues, you must talk to a range of people, not just the leadership team. We will come back to Chloe's situation in a bit.

## GATHERING MULTIPLE PERSPECTIVES

Each human being possesses a unique set of mental maps. No two people interpret reality the same way. For instance, suppose I say the word "lamp." What do you see in your mind's eye? Do you picture a brass banker's desk lamp with a green glass shade, or perhaps a squat black porcelain one that sits on an end table in your living room? Well, the lamp I picture is a stainless-steel arc floor lamp with a Carrara marble base. Many mental maps, many lamps. The same applies to history, as I learned in my first year at university. A disheveled, bespectacled professor pointed out that no two historians report an event, such as the firebombing of Dresden during World War II, exactly the same way. An account by an American historian will probably present the facts from the victor's point of view, while a German author would most likely write the story from the opposite perspective.

You might be wondering what this has to do with culture work. A lot, it turns out. CEO Linda sees the company's lackluster performance through her lens, while Joshua in accounting, Luisa in HR, and Elliot the janitor all view it from their own unique perspectives. If you want the full picture, you need to look at the culture through many different sets of eyes. Take this little test. How many gold bars do you see (Figure 4.1)?

Linda sees four bars. Elliot sees three. It all depends on where you're standing when you look at the bars.

What exactly do people from the C-suite to the front lines see? Successful change leaders ask that question over and over and over, until they gain a full picture of what's really going on in the organization. To see how this works,

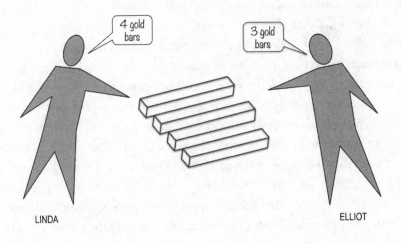

Adapted from image by FB/The Idealist

Figure 4.1. The Number of Gold Bars You
See Depends on Your Perspective

let's return to Chloe Khan as she tries to get a handle on what's hindering her team's performance. You'll recall that she initially attributed it to her supervisors' weak leadership skills. In order to get an objective view of the problem and pinpoint its underlying causes, she invited me to conduct an assessment of her team's culture.

Three weeks later I met with Chloe to go through the findings from the assessment. "What I discovered might surprise you," I began.

She leaned in. "How so?"

"First, some good news. Every one of the senior managers on your team is aligned and agrees that the supervisors are the culprits. The other news? The supervisors blame the managers."

"That hardly surprises me. The supervisors are covering their tails."

"I don't think so. They're angry. And for good reason. One of them summed up their feelings: 'The big bosses just tossed out our old quality policies and procedures without ever seeking our input.'"

Chloe frowned. "That's my fault," she said. "The senior team members felt they needed to act quickly to improve the team's performance, especially with the upcoming work with Metro City. We figured that getting all the supervisors involved would waste valuable time."

"And how did that work out for you?"

She sighed. "Not so good. Our performance stats have been slipping and Fernando is losing patience with my excuses."

We went on to discuss the supervisors' perspective on the performance issues. They were heavily invested in the policies and procedures they had written and refined over the years and felt that the sudden imposition of new rules from above without their input showed a total lack of respect for all the hard work they had done in the past. A dangerous blame game was stalling the change initiative, with senior managers pointing the finger at the supervisors and vice versa. In the end, the supervisors disengaged from their work, resisting the new policies and even sabotaging them in subtle ways. By examining multiple perspectives on the problem, Chloe could finally see the deeper problem, a gulf between the senior team and the supervisors at Waterworks.

Chloe's new insight prompted fresh thinking about the issue. Her first step was to bring the senior managers and the supervisors together to examine the underlying issues that were stalling progress at Waterworks. In this meeting they listened to the results of the culture assessment and got to share their perspectives on what was going wrong in the team. After some initial finger pointing the two sides began to work together to solve the team's issues. Putting the different perspectives on the table helped the supervisors and senior managers to appreciate the alternative views of the situation and to move on to working together to solve their problems. Seeing the different perspectives is often one of the first steps towards solving complex culture problems, that impact multiple parts of a business or team.

I must add a word of caution, however. You should conduct initial interviews and conversations with a promise of strict confidentiality. Otherwise, people may not open up and share their frank opinion about what's happening in the organization. Later, when you bring people together to discuss the problem, you can offer anonymous points of view that will spark honest and open conversations in an atmosphere where people do not fear reprisal for offering negative opinions. It can be easier to discuss some of the complex issues associated with workplace culture, if an independent person (e.g. HR employee or external consultant), puts the topic on the table for discussion.

## ADDING UP THE NUMBERS

Talking to people gives you the "soft" data about what's really going on: the ways of relating between the parts and subjective thoughts and feelings about their colleagues, their work, and the organization. While that provides extremely valuable information about what's happening in the organization, it does not give you everything you need to get the whole story about the current culture. You need to add "hard" data, the facts and figures that give you something to measure. Remember: If you can't measure it, you can't change it. Quantitative information adds a crucial factor to a culture diagnosis, providing hard data to support the qualitative findings.

When Chloe held the workshops to address the productivity issues, she made sure that participants worked on improving the ways of relating between the parts and also kept their eyes on the numbers that would measure progress toward improvement. These metrics included data on water quality, average time to repair burst pipes and leaks, and the reliable flow of water to the city's residents. Business leaders understand that you need yardsticks that show you that you have reduced the defect rate on an assembly line from 22 percent to 1 percent. But many do not realize that they can also measure the (so-called) "soft stuff." Rather than thinking in broad terms that "We need to get everyone more engaged in their work," you should find a yardstick that will tell you whether or not that is happening: "Have we raised our peoples' engagement rate from 22 percent to 86 percent?" "To what extent do our people take the initiative to go above and beyond the strict limits of their job descriptions to solve problems?"

In the case of Waterworks, we conducted an initial employee survey that revealed some interesting numbers about the reasons for the team's poor performance. When asked about the culture, 90 percent of the respondents cited "lack of respect" as an issue, 83 percent listed "cost reduction" as a major problem, and 71 percent and 69 percent respectively mentioned "inflated bureaucracy" and "blaming others for mistakes." The survey also asked people to describe what would make a positive difference in the way they approached their work. More than 85 percent suggested "more open communication," "greater respect," and "more trust" as key factors.

This hard data about the "soft stuff" revealed a big gap between what was going on now and what needed to be going on in the future. I call this gap, culture misalignment. With numbers attached to the current culture at Waterworks, Chloe could set some specific, measurable goals:

- Raise the percentage of people who believe they receive proper respect from 10 percent to 85 percent.
- Increase satisfaction with workplace communication from 15 percent to 85 percent.
- Improve feelings of mutual trust from 15 percent to 85 percent.

Whether you hire an outside consultant or ask your HR team to conduct a culture assessment, make sure that you do not begin to implement a culture change initiative until you have gathered *all* the data you need to make the best possible decisions about what to change and how to change it.

## UNDERSTANDING HOW PEOPLE
## INTERPRET THEIR EXPERIENCES

Human beings naturally wish to make sense of their world. We are sense-making creatures who are constantly gathering data and seeking to make sense of our worlds. Take Sarah (the doctor we met in chapter 1) and her husband Mark, who is a stay-at-home dad. Mark hears their daughter Tara crying in the backyard and he rushes to her aid, because he recognizes the girl's howl of pain. He gives the child's screams meaning: Tara has hurt herself and she needs my help. As Mark runs through the back door, his heart races and his face feels hot. He finds Tara lying on the ground beneath a big oak tree, holding her bleeding knee with both hands. Mark immediately looks for the deeper meaning beneath Tara's cries of pain. Does it mean she has broken her leg or has she just skinned her knee? He examines her cut, "There, there it's just a bad scratch, Tara. I'll get you a band-aid."

Note that this little scenario contains both a rational and an emotional component. All mental maps do. The logical part of Mark's brain works hard to understand the meaning of his daughter's cry for help, while his brain's limbic system ignites strong emotions. He must deal with both. "What is my daughter's medical condition? Stay calm, Mark. You need to keep your wits about you."

Mark is thinking about how he is going to manage the different scenarios that might play out with Tara's injury and he is also connecting to a range of feelings about the situation. Mark continues to scan for new information about his child's condition and to give meaning to this data. This process of making sense of our world, does not stop once people turn up at work. Employees are active agents, not passive receivers of information, who construct and give meaning to what they see and hear in the workplace.

Let's see how meaning-making works in Chloe's maintenance team over at Waterworks. It was the first Christmas after Chloe had started her job and she decided to reward her team with a holiday treat. Wanting to create something truly special, she assembled wicker baskets filled with fresh fruit, cans of smoked almonds, a package of water crackers, a hunk of Wisconsin cheddar, and a bottle of French chardonnay.

Imagine her chagrin when our employee workshops unearthed surprisingly negative feelings about Chloe's extravagant gift. Oscar, a supervisor in one of the recycling plants, spoke for the majority of the team: "We couldn't believe the new boss cancelled the traditional Christmas party. She thought she could buy our loyalty with a basket of stuff we didn't need. We needed that party. Our families looked forward to that event every year. They were so disappointed." Of the team, it turned out that 75 percent thought (and felt) that Chloe did not care about them and their families.

Chloe wanted to create one mental map ("I appreciate you guys"), while her team developed quite a different one ("Chloe doesn't really care about us"). What a gap! Had Chloe taken time to learn about her team's traditions, she would have held the Christmas party, rather than giving team members lavish gift baskets.

As you diagnose your current culture, make sure you understand the meaning that people are giving to their experiences at work. What meaning do your people ascribe to events at work? What do people *think* about their work, their colleagues, and the organization? What makes them *feel* good? What makes them *feel* bad? You must know the answers to such questions *before* you launch a culture change initiative.

## SEEING THE BIG PATTERNS

In chapter 2, I used a spiderweb as an analogy for workplace culture. The individual threads of the web are the behaviors but it is the pattern that connects these different strands. You must see the web (the pattern) as well as the individual threads (the behaviors). Unlike the clearly visible pattern of a spiderweb hanging from a branch in the garden, a culture's patterns are not always so easy to see.

As I've mentioned earlier, Sarah and Mark Connors have nine-year-old twins, Tara and Ethan. Mark is a stay-at-home dad and he gets fed up with picking up the kids' toys and dirty clothes scattered over the carpet in their bedrooms. "I've told you guys a million times to put your toys away and put your dirty clothes in the laundry hamper. I'm sick and tired of picking up after you." Mark feels resentful. The kids hate to hear him complaining all the time. And nothing changes.

Let's examine what's going on here. Who should we blame, the kids for their continued bad behavior, or the parents for not teaching them to do better? The answer: Mark (as the stay-at-home dad) and his children have entered into an unspoken agreement that "dad will pick up the toys and laundry from the bedroom floor." No matter how loudly Mark admonishes, no matter how angry he gets, nothing changes because he does not see the big pattern: his role as a co-creator of this pattern of the twins not taking responsibility for keeping their rooms tidy. Mark has stepped into the role of "picker upper," while the twins are the "clothes droppers" (Figure 4.2).

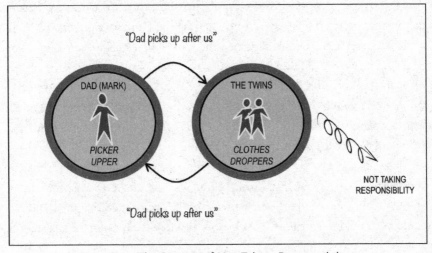

Figure 4.2. The Pattern of Not Taking Responsibility

Nothing will change until Mark sees a pattern that defies easy detection. This applies to workplace culture.

*Nothing will change until you see the big patterns.*

In the case of Chloe's maintenance team, we collected a ton of data about the culture by observing and talking with people, convening focused workshops, and conducting a comprehensive employee survey. The findings prompted Chloe to ask, "Who shoulders the blame for our performance issues: the senior team, the supervisors, or the workers? What is the root cause of the problem?" Good questions, right? Actually, no. Those questions assume that there is one, singular cause of the problem. In culture work there is never a single root cause. Culture is always cocreated.

"Wait a minute," you might be thinking to yourself. "I thought you and Chloe were looking for the root cause?" No, I don't think in terms of root cause. Managers are often told, "Analyze the issue and get to the single, source of the problem!" In culture work we are not looking for a root cause—instead we must learn to see the connected patterns and the role different parts play in co-creating them.

When Chloe and I examined the web revealed by all that data, we realized that the senior managers had shown disregard for the supervisors by throwing out the policy documents and cancelling the Christmas party. For their part, the supervisors had disregarded the senior managers by accusing them of incompetence and failing to step in to help employees make sense of the new work procedures. See the pattern here? The managers and the supervisors were signaling to each other that, "You don't know, and you don't care." This cocreated pattern (shown in Figure 4.3) was running the maintenance team and negatively impacting performance.

This diagram really opened Chloe's eyes. She could see that sending the supervisors to a leadership-training seminar would not solve the problem. It would do nothing to alter the big pattern that governed the situation. In fact, it could make matters worse. The supervisors would be likely to see the instruction

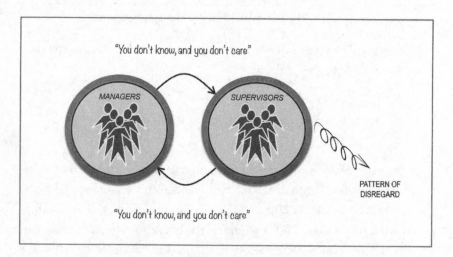

Figure 4.3. The Pattern of Disregard

to attend leadership classes as yet another example of senior management's disregard for their skills and experience, thus reinforcing the big pattern.

Seeing the pattern led Chloe to take a different approach to solving the culture problem. We will detail her solution when we get to that step on The Culture Disruptor. Meanwhile, let's look at one more example of big pattern detection.

You will recall that the managers at BuildItPro, the infrastructure business we met earlier, were strongly resisting changes to the way they did their work. While the market had shifted to highly specific and tightly controlled contracts under which managers could not offer unlimited free help to clients, BuildItPro's people could not set that practice aside. The company was hemorrhaging red ink because the contracts had not built in a contingency for the cost of work, beyond the signed agreement, and BuildItPro staff were doing additional work without charging.

Who can blame the managers for wanting to keep playing Mr. and Ms. Nice Guy/Gal? It had always worked so well. It made them feel good, and it made clients happy. "You want an extra pipe laid? We'll get right on it! You want us to fix a machine that's no longer under warranty? No problem! Tear down that wall and put up another wall a foot away? Of course!" It was all unicorns and rainbows, except for the people at headquarters who had to pay a lot of unexpected bills.

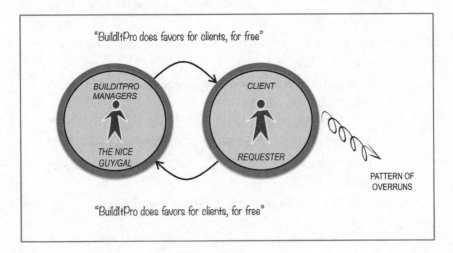

Figure 4.4. The Pattern of Overruns

Take a look at the big pattern BuildItPro's leaders needed to see (Figure 4.4):

Of course, the clients and BuildItPro managers who had cocreated that pattern fought to keep it in place. Changing it would cause too much angst. So what should BuildItPro's CEO, Ben Harkness, do? Send his managers to finance school? That would not address the big pattern. Instead, he needed to deal directly with the pattern of doing costly favors for clients. As with Chloe's crew at Waterworks, we will see what Ben at BuildItPro decided to do when we get to that step on The Culture Disruptor.

Nothing will more quickly ruin a major change effort than a failure to see the patterns that govern how people relate to each other in the organization. In most organizations, the big patterns have become almost invisible. One of the main objectives of this first step, *Diagnose*, on The Culture Disruptor is to make the patterns visible. Failure to identify the big patterns at this stage, can mean that you take a wrong turn early on in the change journey. Once you correctly identify the patterns, you can greatly increase your chances of putting the right solutions in place that deal with the underlying issues (not the symptoms).

### · POINTS TO REMEMBER ·

- Leaders can begin to diagnose what's going on by walking around the workplace.
- Astute change leaders resist the temptation to jump (too quickly) to solutions.
- The full picture emerges only when you gather information from multiple perspectives.
- Even the "soft stuff" can be quantified and measured.
- A successful change effort depends on finding the big patterns that govern the way the parts relate to each other in the organization.
- Patterns are always cocreated and can be difficult to detect.

# 5

## REFRAME
## THE ROLES

### Turning Everyone in the
### Organization into a Change Leader

In 1971, Philip Zimbardo, a professor of psychology at Stanford University, conducted the controversial psychological study that became known as the Stanford Prison Experiment. To explore the interactions of guards and prisoners, Professor Zimbardo set up a simulated prison environment in the basement of the university's psychology department, and then placed advertisements in the campus newspaper asking for male volunteers, eventually selecting twenty-four college students to play the key roles in the experiment.

Wanting to lend as much reality to the scenario as possible, the professor arranged for the local Palo Alto police department to "arrest" the would-be prisoners at their homes and charge them with armed robbery. With chains bolted to their ankles, the "prisoners" wore official-looking numbered uniforms and stocking caps, while the "guards" sported crisp khaki uniforms, a whistle, a baton, and mirrored sunglasses to prevent eye contact. Zimbardo himself played the role of "superintendent," imposing ground rules that prohibited physical violence or withholding food and water.

Despite the rules, it did not take long for the make-believe play to take a grim turn. Within twenty-four hours, some of the guards began to abuse the prisoners, conducting surprise roll calls at 2:00 a.m., forcing prisoners to memorize their prison numbers, and ordering them to perform push-ups. The prisoners responded by barricading themselves in their cells and taunting the guards. The guards, upset by such resistance to their authority, stripped the prisoners naked, removed their beds, and forced them to wear paper bags on their heads. They even threw the rebellious leader into solitary confinement for his defiant behavior.

The behaviors grew so extreme that Zimbardo halted the experiment after only six days. The results of the disturbing study, according to Zimbardo, indicated that "situational factors" had an impact on behavior. In my view, it also pointed to the impact of role: Men who were assigned the role of "tough prison guard" took up that role, some more brutally than others. The males who were assigned to the role of "powerless prisoner" also stepped into this role and became submissive.

The college students in Zimbardo's experiment reframed (or adjusted) their role from "students" to "guards/prisoners." This role reframe led to immediate shifts in their behavior. The shocking study raised many questions, but also pointed to the potential impact of role expectations on behavior.

Although the prisoner case study above has negative connotations, it also illustrates how powerful role expectations might be, if used in a positive way. Leaders can use the reframing technique to accelerate change, during culture transformation. This brings us to the second step, *Reframe* your role, on The Culture Disruptor (Figure 5.1). This step is symbolized by a pair of glasses, indicating that how you see or frame the roles (at work), can lead to rapid shifts in behavior.

## KNOWING WHAT YOU CAN
## AND CANNOT CHANGE

One popular approach to altering behavior in the workplace addresses personality rather than role. Rebecca, a call center worker, reacts angrily when-

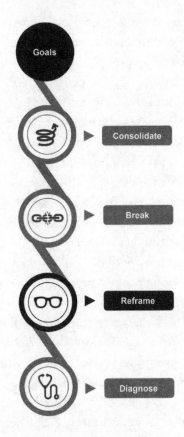

Figure 5.1. The Second Step on The Culture Disruptor: Reframe the Roles

ever a customer asks for an exception to her company's returns policy. Send her to an anger management counselor? That may work to some extent, but in my experience, you can make a deeper and more lasting change by modifying her role from "policy enforcer" to "customer advocate." Let me explain.

There are three major influences on how we are wired to behave: instincts, personality, and role. Researchers tell us that we all possess powerful instincts that have evolved over millions of years. These include the instinct for survival, an instinct to connect with fellow human beings, and an instinct to protect our offspring. These drivers of human behavior have been so hard-wired into our brains that we find it almost impossible to counteract them. Rebecca has a deeply wired instinct to feed and protect her family. She may fear that a failure to enforce the company's policy returns, could cost her the job at the call center. Her instinct to protect her family may lead her to fight hard against any request for an exception to the returns policy.

The second factor that may be influencing Rebecca's behavior is her personality. Her environment since birth has shaped the way she responds to certain situations. She has developed a unique personality. While you or I may have learned to handle a difficult person with gracious understanding and forgiveness, Rebecca has developed a tendency to react with impatience and aggression. Personality traits cover the full range of human behavior, such as gregariousness, introversion, kindness, generosity, honesty, calm acceptance, a hair-trigger temper, and countless others. As with instincts, people find it quite difficult to modify their personality, especially in challenging situations. If Rebecca grew up with three older, domineering brothers, she may have developed a strong inclination to fight back whenever she thinks someone is trying to take advantage of her.

That brings us to role. We all carry around mental maps of the multiple roles we take up every day. Remember the doctor, Sarah Connors—in any one day she might take up multiple roles, including wife, parent, commuter, medical professional, department head, work colleague, basketball coach, and homework reviewer. Like the GPS in a car, her mental map of the role she is taking up at any given point in time, helps her to navigate her way through these role changes. If and when Sarah's path shifts in other directions, such as when she changes her career or her marital status, or any other major element in her life, she can update it by adding to or reframing her role.

We all use mental maps to guide our behavior. These maps define our roles and tell us how to act in various situations. If Rebecca's boss, Eleanor, has expected her to play the role of "policy enforcer," she will develop a mental map that governs the way she plays that role, causing her to resist any request for an exception to her company's returns policy by a customer, no matter how legitimate the request.

Now suppose that Eleanor wants Rebecca to handle customer requests with less rigidity and without getting angry if customers persist in their demands. Should she try to change Rebecca's instinct to protect her job at all costs? Should she try to encourage Rebecca to develop a totally different personality? No, Eleanor may be able to bring about a swifter change by reframing Rebecca's role to "customer advocate." Thinking of her role in this way, is likely to lead Rebecca to behave in a different way to the "policy enforcer." Role expectations are typically easier to change, than working with hardwired instincts or personality (Figure 5.2).

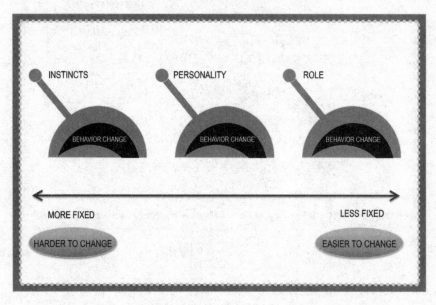

Figure 5.2. Three Levers for Changing Behavior

When you decide to change your organization's culture, it is often advisable to avoid trying to tackle hardwired instincts or asking people to change their personalities. Instead, focus on what you can more easily and more quickly change: the roles that guide people's behavior in your workplace.

So where should you begin reframing roles? It usually makes sense to start at the top, and then work your way down the levels of the organization (Figure 5.3):

1. Leader (boss)
2. Leadership group (team)
3. Business units
4. All employees

Compare it to a football team. If you want to field a championship team, you want to hire a management team that thinks and acts like "talent recruiters." The

REFRAMING ROLES FROM THE TOP DOWN

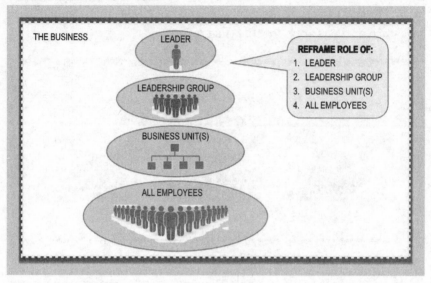

Figure 5.3. Top-Down Role Reframing

management team hire a head coach to play the role of "performance en-hancer." The head coach assembles a group of assistant coaches who serve as "skills trainers," teaching and inspiring the players to play like "championship contenders." Even the junior employees on the sidelines think of themselves as "attendants to champions" rather than the mere "watergirls" or "waterboys."

## TAKING UP YOUR ROLE AS CHANGE LEADER

Over the past thirty years, I have asked dozens of senior leaders to describe how they view their role within the business. The responses have included:

- Exceed customer expectations.
- Deliver greater returns to shareholders.
- Grow the business faster than our competitors.
- Continuously improve results.
- Provide more opportunities for employee growth and development.

These executives did not describe their change role, despite the fact that they were presiding over major transformation efforts in their organizations. This begs the question, "How can you expect a change initiative to succeed if you do not define your role as the 'chief change officer'?" Of course, all leaders must maintain a mental map that guides their daily work with respect to the basic requirements of running a business, but they must add to that map their role to lead the business from an old to a new culture, if necessary (Figure 5.4).

It's always tempting to keep on doing what you have always done, perhaps spending all your time attending to pressing business demands or putting out fires, but when you embark on a change effort, you must put your change initiative at the top of your daily to-do list. In my experience, that means devoting at least 20 percent of your time to leading and overseeing the change agenda, especially in the early days.

*Transformational leaders spend at least 20 percent of their time taking up their change role.*

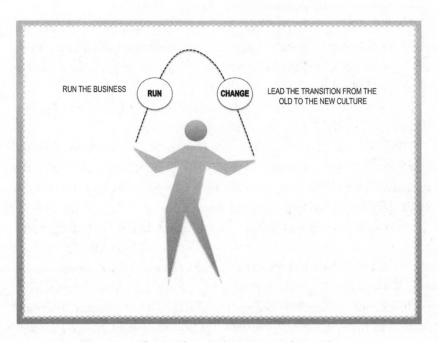

Figure 5.4. The Leader's Role During Culture Change

At one point in my career, I worked as a change advisor to the CEO of a nationwide supermarket chain. The CEO, "Paul Lee," had successfully run "Big Value" for ten years and had always tried to stay a few steps ahead of his rivals. To that end, he had begun a huge digital transformation project designed to give customers a state-of-the-art online shopping experience. I had barely sat down in his office, when he launched into a list of serious problems with the initiative. "I've poured $20 million into this digital project, because I know that the right online presence will attract and hold customers, but nothing has changed. 'Fresh Guys,' our number one competitor, is still gaining market share. When I look at our online shopping experience, our social media marketing, and our analytics capability, our progress seems to be moving at a glacial pace."

I asked Paul to share his vision for Big Value's future. He responded, "I told our people on day one that I want our online world to address the fact that customer tastes have changed, that they want new products that better match their lifestyles. Customers demand the sort of local, seasonal products they find on our competitors' shelves. We are not anticipating and meeting our customers' needs, and our online offerings reflect that."

I suspected the problem. "Paul, you said 'on day one.' May I assume that you gave your digital team its marching orders, then turned them loose to achieve your objective of creating a more customer-centric culture while you went back to your usual duties as CEO?"

He shot me a puzzled look. "Of course! I hire the best people. I expect them to do the job without constant supervision."

"Well, I'm not suggesting they need constant supervision, but even the brightest stars need an involved leader to keep promoting and guiding the mission. Without daily contact with their change leader, a great team can easily slip into the old way of doing things."

Paul closed his eyes and sighed. "I *know* that. I do it with strategic initiatives every day. Why didn't I do it with our culture? Don't answer that. I get it now." Six months later, I revisited Big Value. Paul invited me to sit in on his weekly digital meeting, where he asked questions, gave a lot of appreciative feedback, and repeated his mantra: "Big Value Is the Supermarket of Tomorrow." After the meeting, he showed me the bottom-line results. "We've made online shopping available in all major cities, and we are using advanced analytics to predict what customers want to buy today and in the future. Using this information, we have created social media campaigns based on what customers will love. As a result, sales are up 17 percent."

## TURNING THE LEADERSHIP GROUP INTO CHANGE LEADERS

We have been following the story of CEO Ben Harkness' effort to create a new high-performing, innovative, and cost-conscious culture at BuildItPro. Six months after he launched the initiative, a mid-course culture checkup revealed a good deal of backsliding into old habits. He described an unsettling teleconference call with his top one hundred executives. "Siobhan, I've gotta tell you, I did 90 percent of the talking, and I got the sinking feeling everyone was sitting on the other end of the line just waiting for me to shut up so they could get back to business as usual."

This did not surprise me. "You've stepped up as a leader, but you're letting your team play the role of observers. You need to break that pattern. And the way you can do it is to change their roles to coleaders of the change campaign" (Figure 5.5).

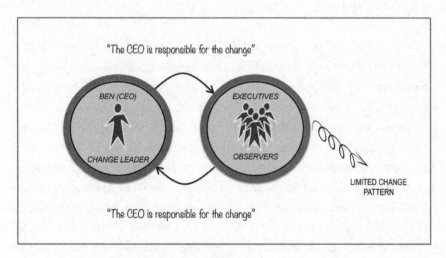

Figure 5.5. A Disengaged Leadership Group

Realizing that he needed to reframe his team's roles in the change effort, Ben invited his top one hundred leaders to a two-day change conference where he addressed the issue head-on. "You are leaders, not followers. We can't expect our people to adopt new practices if you do not act like leaders. No one but me said a word about our change initiative during our last teleconference." He showed them my sketch depicting the CEO leading a team of observers. "We've got to change this picture," He crossed out the word "observers" and wrote "change leaders" in its place. "I want you to think like change leaders, talk like change leaders, and act like change leaders" (Figure 5.6).

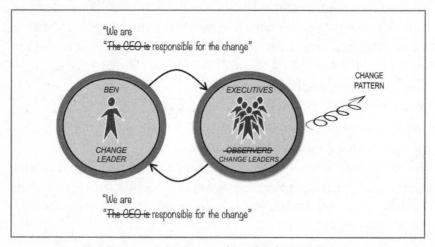

Figure 5.6. An Engaged Leadership Group

Finally the CEO could hear his leadership group singing the same tune: "What can *we* do to make BuildItPro a more innovative, cost-conscious, and more productive and profitable company?" By reframing the role of his leadership group, he had taken a crucial step on the change journey.

Ben was learning a key change lesson: that a single, visionary leader cannot carry all of the responsibility for change. Even the most capable leader can't lead culture change alone. She needs the support of a committed leadership group, working together on the transformation agenda. Every member of the leadership team must reframe their role to "change leader" in order to deliver the change.

Successful change leaders understand the power of getting leadership alignment when it comes to the change agenda. The best leaders work hard to do that. In one notable case, William Bratton helped create an astonishing transformation of New York's transit system in the early 1990s. For decades prior to Bratton's appointment, passengers dreaded riding the subway cars that rumbled beneath the streets of New York. Graffiti covered the walls of the stations and the cars, young thugs blocked turnstiles and demanded protection money from passengers, and drug addicts and alcoholics used the platforms as their bedrooms and bathrooms. I know. I rode the system to and from work for a few months in the late 1980s. I literally feared for my life. So did the dwindling number of people who kept using the system. The transit system was losing passengers and their fares at an alarming rate.

Despite these conditions, the leaders of the New York City Transit Authority were slow to grasp the need for change. After all, New York was a dangerous place, and only 3 percent of the city's major crimes occurred on the subway. Nevertheless, they did order the removal of graffiti along the subway routes. Unfortunately, clean walls did not solve the problem. When Bratton began his new job as head of New York's Transit Police in 1990, he faced a daunting task. On September 2, 1990, a twenty-two-year-old Utah resident named Brian Watkins, accompanied by his parents, brother, and sister-in-law, had entered the New York City subway system in Midtown, looking forward to dinner at the famous Tavern on the Green restaurant after a short subway ride. A group of teenagers surrounded the Watkins family on the subway platform, beat the mother and father, and stabbed young Brian to death. The attackers used the money they stole to buy tickets to the nearby Roseland Ballroom. Watkins's death was the eighteenth of twenty-six murders in New York's subways in 1990, and further proof that change was an imperative.

Bratton saw this imperative and boldly addressed the safety problem by insisting that all transit police officers, including him, make their presence felt in the public transit system. The officers could see and feel and smell the problems besetting the system and committed themselves to the cause: "We have *got* to change this!" They quickly developed a zero tolerance culture that waged an all-out war to make the subway system safe for passengers.

Toward the end of Bratton's first year as Transit Police chief, misdemeanor arrests rose 80 percent, with felonies declining precipitously. In 1990, transit riders were victims of 17,497 felonies, including murders, robberies, rapes, assaults, and thefts. Two years later, the number had dropped to 12,199. As proactive policing continued, the subways got safer. According to the *New York Post*, by 2000, felonies had plunged to 4,263, and in 2015, the figure fell to 2,502. New York's subway system now serves more passengers than at any time since World War II. New Yorkers, visitors, and commuting workers take nearly 1.8 billion annual trips, nearly double the number in 1980.

I connect with this story, not only because I can personally relate to it, but also because it perfectly illustrates my point that a successful change effort is a joint endeavor in which everyone on the management team must think and act as change leaders.

## MOBILIZING BUSINESS UNITS TO CHANGE

Astute change leaders reframe the role of entire business units in order to accelerate the change effort. Employees in business units tend to develop a shared a mental map of the role that they take up within the organization. Transformational leaders adjust these business unit roles, in order to bring about faster change. Patrick Houlihan, the CEO at the paints and hardware company DuluxGroup, skillfully reframed his company's R&D unit. Patrick took over as CEO when the company was spun off from its parent company, Orica, in 2010. The company employed more than 140 chemists in the R&D department as a means of keeping DuluxGroup at the leading edge of new product development in the markets the company served. Patrick's analysis of the R&D unit's culture revealed that the chemists saw their role as "technical experts," tasked with providing formulations for paints, sealants, and adhesive products. This mental map had remained in place for more than thirty years, even before Houlihan himself had joined the company as a junior chemist in R&D, and it had worked very well for the company up until now.

Future growth and success, Houlihan decided, would require the chemists to think of themselves as "product innovators." To accomplish that shift in thinking, we conducted a series of intensive workshops with the company's R&D leaders aimed at helping them reframe their role as "innovators." Houlihan encouraged them by declaring, "I want consumers to say 'wow!' when they see our products!"

Fast-forward twelve months, and the R&D department was indeed wowing consumers with new products like Storm, a quick-setting filler contractors and homeowners could use to fix gaps in roofs, even in the pouring rain. Storm quickly became a bestseller in its category.

Successful change leaders realize that members of a business unit must replace current mental maps with new ones that support the change initiative. The simple act of reframing can help everyone pivot in the right direction during culture transformation. ANZ bank's John McFarlane, recognizing the pattern of blame that infected two of the company's business units, decided to change them both (Figure 5.7).

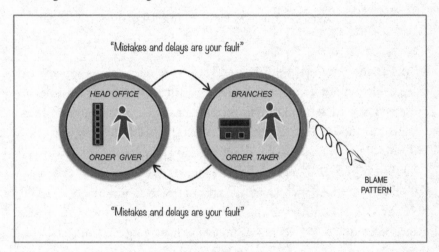

Figure 5.7. The Old Blame Pattern

The CEO reframed the role of head office from "order giver" to "support giver." This sent a clear message: "Your job is to help the branches deliver better service to customers."

He also reframed the role of those working in the branches from "order takers" to "service deliverers." This sent another clear message: "Your job is to anticipate and meet the needs of our customers and the communities we serve."

Reframing the roles created a new pattern between branches and head office from "Mistakes and errors are your fault" to "We work together to serve the customer" (Figure 5.8).

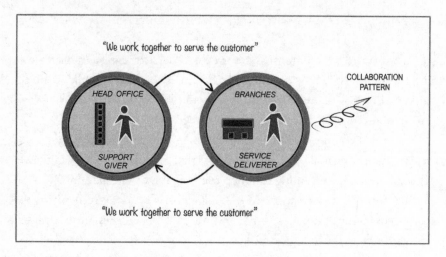

Figure 5.8. The New Pattern of Collaboration

McFarlane reframed both business units to accelerate company-wide change. He did not leave it to his HR department to reframe the roles, because he knew he needed to reinforce the change message himself. In too many companies, senior executives leave what they see as the "soft stuff" up to HR, shirking accountability for the change. That always ends in disaster.

During my first week at BuildItPro, I met with the company's chief financial officer, "Asad Ali," who had offered to brief me about the dire need to stem the tide of company losses. "We've had ongoing issues with performance on contracts. Project managers are not managing their budgets, which is contributing to company losses. Our shareholders are furious, and the organization urgently needs a higher performing culture if we are to survive in a more competitive world." Clearly, he saw the need for change. As we shook hands at the end of the meeting, Asad offered a few parting words: "*Good luck with the culture change.*"

I immediately realized that the CFO saw my role as the lone agent of change. I paused at the door, and then sat back down to explore this misconception. It turned out that, before I arrived, HR had guided an earlier change initiative aimed at improving performance. When results failed to materialize after several months, HR ramped up its change efforts, conducting more workshops and events and sending out a flurry of focused communications.

That also failed to get results. All the time, line managers sat on the sidelines, waiting and hoping for HR to succeed. Eventually, the CEO abandoned the initiative. Perhaps a new culture change expert would do a better job. That's when I came aboard. I knew that my efforts would also fail if line managers placed total responsibility for change on my shoulders.

When I met with CEO Ben Harkness to discuss the situation, he immediately understood the problem. At an initial change conference with BuildIt-Pro's senior leaders, he reframed the roles of HR and the company's other leaders. "HR will be a major 'change enabler,' providing advice, tools, and training to fast-track our progress, but you must never forget that each of us is a 'change leader.'" Within twelve months, Asad Ali happily reported measurable progress toward a more accountable and financially responsible organization.

## ALIGNING EMPLOYEES WITH THE MISSION

Do you think of yourself as an employee? The word suggests a certain pecking order that separates leaders from workers. During transformational change employees must be invited to make the change happen within their areas of responsibility. In the context of a culture change initiative, everyone, from the chairman of the board to the janitor, must adopt the role of "change leader."

Patrick Houlihan, the leader of DuluxGroup we met earlier in this chapter, understood the power of enrolling all employees in the change agenda. When Patrick took over as CEO in 2010, he launched a campaign stressing the newly designed values that framed the role of all employees to "run the business as your own." To prove his commitment to that way of thinking about your job, he gave all his people the opportunity to own shares in the company.

By 2015, however, a careful analysis of the DuluxGroup culture revealed that his people were focused more on running the business than growing the business. Patrick decided to change that. He started with a program called "Grow and Think Beyond" that reframed the role of his people as "Growth Enablers" as well as "Deliverers." He expected them not only to run the business but to grow the business by creating new products and entering new markets.

Four years later, Patrick was seeing significant progress, especially when word of the amazing growth-oriented culture at DuluxGroup reached some folks who were looking to buy a major Australian company. In April 2019, the Japanese firm Nippon Paint Holdings (the fourth largest paint company in the world) swooped in with an offer to buy the company at a remarkable price of $9.80 per share (versus the $2.50 share price when the company was listed at the time of demerger in 2010). This was the highest price ever offered for a paint company anywhere in the world (16.1 times EBITDA—earnings before interest, tax, depreciation, and amortization). This accomplishment provided incontrovertible proof of Houlihan's ability to reframe the roles of his employees in order to create a culture that could deliver, grow, and adapt.

Houlihan knew the power of getting his people onto the same page of the change agenda. When the leaders at Nordstrom, the upscale department store, wanted to engage employees in their quest to create a truly customer-centric culture, they also redefined their role. But rather than producing a binder with hundreds of pages describing the behaviors the company's leaders thought would make this happen, they formulated one simple rule. Showcased in the employee handbook, this rule reframed the role that each Nordstrom employee should play in the culture:

*Rule #1: Use good judgment in all situations.*
*There will be no additional rules.*

This rule of "good judgment in all situations" invited employees to move from the role of "shop assistant" to the role of "business owner." Rather than merely assisting customers with their purchases, Nordstrom's people should *own* the outcome.

This reframed role immediately influenced people to go out of their way to eliminate the pain points for customers. As "business owners," they began to look with fresh eyes at their customers' experience shopping at Nordstrom, from what customers saw the moment they entered the store to their experience with their purchases at home. You hear a phone ringing? Answer it before the third ring. A customer asks where he can find children's clothes? You escort him to that department. You have just wrapped a bulky sweater for a customer? You walk around the counter and hand it to them, or, even better, you offer to carry it to their car. It did not take long for the good judgment rule to earn Nordstrom a reputation as a provider of unparalleled service and a destination-of-choice for shoppers. It was not your same old department store. It was the store where customers got personalized service.

Nordstrom's leaders found a simple yet powerful way to attract and hold customers far more effectively than once-dominant retailers such as J. C. Penny and Sears, which faltered and fell by the wayside in the fierce competition for shoppers' dollars.

Underscore the word *simple*. Anyone hoping to engineer a culture change should summarize new roles in clear, concise, and compelling terms. You might recognize the Boy Scout motto: Be Prepared. Rather than suggesting that boys behave properly, the motto (or call it "the reframed role") reminds them of the values that should guide their every action.

### Being Prepared

The Scout motto "Be Prepared" means remaining ready to do whatever you can to help others, It also means that a good Scout prepares to react quickly and effectively to each and every one of life's challenges. From those two simple words springs a whole set of tenets that help a Scout live a full and worthwhile life as a physically fit, honorable citizen with a strong character.

Can you craft a word or short sentence that captures the role you want your people to play in the change initiative? Don't settle for the first one that pops into your head. It takes time to write a truly great one. Bear in mind Mark Twain's apology for sending a long-winded letter to a friend: "I would have made it shorter, if I'd had the time."

You can reframe roles in multiple ways. At Southwest Airlines, CEO Herb Kelleher defined the company's expectations of employees in three organizational values:

1. A warrior spirit. Be fearless in delivering service to customers.
2. A servant's heart. Connect with people, treat them with respect, and put their needs first, with friendly and reliable service.

3. A fun-loving attitude. Have fun, enjoy work, and don't take yourself too seriously.

Apple defined the "service" role that its store staff should bring to their interactions with retail customers. The acronym A-P-P-L-E makes it easy for employees to remember the steps:

- Approach customers with a friendly, warm welcome.
- Probe politely to understand all the customer's needs.
- Present the customer with a solution.
- Listen for and resolve any "unexpressed" wishes or concerns.
- End with a warm farewell and an invitation to return.

Google relies on a mission statement to help define the role of employees: "To organize the world's information and make it universally accessible and useful." Susan Wojcicki, Google's senior vice president of advertising, talks about the power of this mission statement to instill desired employee behavior. "We use this simple statement to guide all of our decisions. Our mission is one that has the potential to touch many lives, and we make sure that all our employees feel connected to it and empowered to help achieve it. In times of crisis, they have helped by organizing lifesaving information and making it readily available." For instance, Google's people launched a Person Finder tool within two hours of the 2011 Tohoku earthquake and tsunami that struck northeast Japan.

Let's say you want a customer service team to replace prepared scripts with a question-and-answer approach tailored to each customer who calls to complain about a product your company sells. Do you tell shy Cameron to become a more outgoing and curious person? No, you reframe his role to one of "questioner" and then show him how to ask questions that show empathy for the customer and get to the heart of any dissatisfaction with a product. Cameron does not become more gregarious, but he does learn how to replace his old role of "script reader" with the new role of "questioner." Now he behaves in a way that displays his concern for whatever has upset the customer. "What can I do to help you? Have I answered all your questions? Is there anything more I can do for you?" We each hold a map in our heads that depicts the roles we think we need to take up in various situations, but we seldom write them down or share them with others. You might try this little experiment in role reframing. Write down a role you step into, say "book reader." Then imagine revising your role from "book reader" to "culture researcher." Adding that new role to your map does not mean that you will behave in an inauthentic way. It just means you are choosing to expand your behavior beyond your usual modus operandi. Now, rather than absorbing information about culture, you are thinking of ways you can apply what you are learning to your own change efforts.

What does this have to do with aligning employees with the mission? Roles influence behavior. Stepping into the appropriate roles will prompt people to act in a way that produces desired changes. This basic tenet of effective leadership applies to any effort to change an organization's culture. "But," you may object, "this seems so manipulative, getting people to act in unaccustomed ways, in ways that run counter to their normal behavior."

Not at all. Think about the roles you play in a given week. How do you behave at work, and how does your behavior enable you to do your job? If you work as a sales representative for a medical company, you dress and act in ways that help you build good relationships with the physicians you visit. Are you married or single? If you go out to a bar for a drink after work, you would behave one way if you hope to meet your future partner, and another way if you are going home to your spouse. If you work out at a gym or play a competitive sport, such as golf or tennis, you behave in ways that suit those activities. Now, suppose I ask you to help me deal with an emergency, perhaps helping people who have just survived a train wreck. Basically, I might be asking you to take up a role you've never played in your life. But you would probably try to step into this role and act in a way that meets the demands of this situation.

Over the course of her busy week, the usually calm and reserved Sarah Connors, the head of cardiology at Mount Sinai Hospital, could step into any number of roles. If she comes upon an automobile accident on her way to the train station, she immediately becomes a first responder, issuing orders in a firm, commanding voice she would never use with her staff at work. She's still her normally calm and reserved self, but she has adopted an entirely different role of "first responder" in this emergency. So it goes with culture change. A leader doesn't ask people to become different people. She makes it clear that she needs them to take up a new role in order to deal with the current "emergency." Think for a moment about John McFarlane's situation at ANZ bank. He faced a challenge that anyone would have called an emergency. In a sense, then, a culture change is often a response to a form of organizational emergency. Otherwise, why bother?

## · POINTS TO REMEMBER ·

- Reframing roles will bring about faster change.
- You can accelerate change by reframing four key roles: the boss, the leadership group, business units, and all employees.
- Effective leaders spend at least 20 percent of their time in their change leader role.
- HR cannot take sole responsibility for bringing about the change.
- Employees, at all levels, must take up their role as change leaders.
- Keep it simple. Summarize the role in a clear, concise, and compelling phrase or sentence.

# 6

## TAKE CHARGE
## OF THE JOURNEY

### Becoming an Inspiring
### Change Leader

Ben Harkness, the CEO of BuildItPro, the underperforming infrastructure company we discussed earlier in this book, had grown impatient with the change initiative designed to create a more productive and commercial culture. "We're trying to become leaner and meaner, but we're just getting fatter and slower," he complained me in one of our regular catchups. "We can't even get that new billboard up on the roof." To promote BuildItPro's new brand, the marketing department had designed a beautiful image of speeding race cars that would show the world that the company had become a highly responsive and productive enterprise. Although he had approved the design four months earlier, the advertising billboard still hadn't appeared on the rooftop. Ben shared his frustration with everyone but Henry Tucker, BuildItPro's head of marketing. He didn't want to have the difficult conversation with Henry.

I stepped into my role as Ben's coach. I suggested that, by not giving feedback to Henry about the billboard delay, he may have been fueling the pattern of poor performance in the company. Ben got it immediately, "Yes, I've got to lead by example and stop playing Mr. Nice Guy." That day, he pulled together his executive team and opened the meeting with a little speech about holding the necessary conversations about BuildItPro's problems. "Henry, where is that billboard?" A lively discussion ensued. At the end, Henry promised he would get it done by the end of the week. Everyone who attended that meeting took the message about candid conversations back to their people.

> *Leaders must break the deeply*
> *embedded patterns in the culture.*

Ben was beginning to realize that culture change never happens until the leader steps up to break the prevailing patterns in the old culture. Leaders cannot simply stand on the sidelines and observe the journey. Their behaviors can either serve to fuel the old culture, or bring about a change to the new ways. If you take up the role of the business-as-usual boss, people may pay lip service to change and keep on doing what they have always done. Step into the role of change boss, and you can inspire people to get on board with the transformation. This brings us to the third step of on The Culture Disruptor, *Break* the patterns (Figure 6.1).

Patterns are at the heart of workplace culture. When it comes to breaking old patterns, it helps to study how other leaders have done it. The automobile industry offers three excellent cases in point.

## LEARNING FROM PATTERN-BREAKING LEADERS

Henry Ford, born in 1863 on a farm in Wayne County, Michigan, created an enterprise that would grow into one of the largest automobile manufacturers and most recognized brands in the world. As a boy, Henry loved tinkering with the pocket watch his father gave him, taking it apart to examine how it

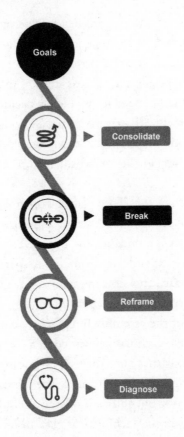

Figure 6.1. The Third Step on The Culture Disruptor: Break the Patterns

operated. That tinkering, and his budding head for business, helped him become a sought-after watch repairer in his local area. At age sixteen, he left the farm and moved to nearby Detroit, where he secured a job as a machinist. While Ford's mechanical talents propelled him to a position as chief engineer at the Edison Illuminating Company, the young entrepreneur dreamed of "putting the world on wheels."

In 1903, Henry started the Ford Motor Company with $28,000 in cash collected from twelve investors. During the early days of production in his Highland Park factory, Ford built cars, one at a time, just like everybody else. Groups of two or three men gathered around the chassis as it sat on the ground, running off occasionally to acquire needed parts. This method produced just a few cars a day.

Wishing to speed production, Ford began experimenting with the process, first transferring the chassis to benches where assemblers could more easily work on the vehicles. Then he moved the benches from team to team, initiating the idea of specialists in various steps of the process. That didn't satisfy Ford. How could he speed it up? Henry decided to make the larger parts of the chassis himself with new machines, allowing workers to put them in place much faster. Still, it took much too long to produce the final product. Then Ford made one of the most brilliant breakthroughs in business history.

In his Highland Park factory, Ford placed workers at fixed stations where they could perform their assigned tasks while a strong rope pulled the chassis along the line. It may seem mundane now, but the assembly line revolutionized manufacturing in every industry from toys to space stations. The assembly line did not just make it possible to manufacture gizmos much faster; it created a whole new type of workplace culture.

Before the advent of the assembly line, factory employees worked in a loose-knit culture where each worker served as a sort of jack-of-all-trades, performing whatever task that came their way—bolting on a wheel for a few minutes, then installing a window the next. The job may not have inspired them to do excellent work, but at least it offered a certain amount of variety. Now, standing at the wheel attachment or glass installation station all day long, performing a single task over and over and over again, made the work almost robotic. (Ironically, robots would, in fact, one day replace many of the humans who worked on assembly lines.)

The assembly-line technique transformed the American national culture. Decreased costs of production, passed on to the consumer, afforded the average American middle-class family a swift means of transportation. At the same time, it transformed workplace culture with higher wages for repetitive and monotonous work. In 1908, a Ford Model T sold for around $825; by 1912, the price had fallen to around $575 (comparable to a reduction of $15,000 in today's dollars); and by 1914, an assembly-line worker could buy a Model T with four months' pay.

Ford's complex safety procedures, such as assigning workers to specific locations instead of allowing them to roam about the shop floor, dramatically reduced the rate of injury. The combination of high wages and high efficiency, dubbed "Fordism," became the norm in industries around the world. Workers took pride in their jobs, brought home hefty paychecks, and remained deeply loyal to their employer. Their mental maps defined a new role for workers and a new pattern of relating in the world of manufacturing (Figure 6.2).

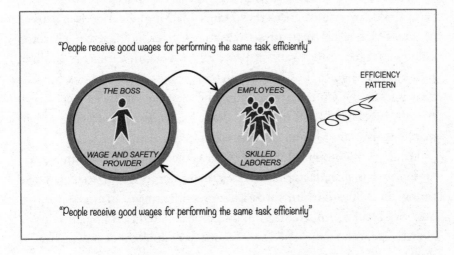

"People receive good wages for performing the same task efficiently"

THE BOSS

EMPLOYEES

EFFICIENCY
PATTERN

WAGE AND SAFETY
PROVIDER

SKILLED
LABORERS

"People receive good wages for performing the same task efficiently"

Figure 6.2. Assembly-Line Culture

The next wave of culture change in the automotive industry occurred in post-war Japan, where W. Edwards Deming, an American working as a management consultant, helped transform Toyota into a dominant force. Deming, born near 1900 in Polk City, Iowa, moved on from his farming community to become a world-class engineer, statistician, professor, and quality-control guru. Although his ideas about manufacturing quality went largely unheeded in America, they found fertile ground in a decimated postwar Japan in the 1950s.

Japanese industrialists, eager to rebuild their country by exporting top quality products that would beat US manufacturers at their own game, listened intently to Deming's sermons on quality. Until then, Americans poked fun at Japanese cars like Toyota's hapless Toyopet Crown, a heavy, slow dinosaur unsuited to American highways and the American appetite for speed and power.

Toyota's leaders went back to the drawing board with Deming's quality mantra ringing in their ears. Deming delivered a simple central message: "Do it right the first time, and do it better the second time." This prompted

Toyota managers to focus on consistent high quality with a relentless drive to eliminate waste and continuously improve every aspect of automobile manufacturing. They applied statistics to the recording of product defects, urged workers to figure out what went wrong, and demanded that everyone work hard to fix even the most minor problem.

In 1957, Toyota introduced the Corona T100 into the American market. This new car boasted many attractive features: available as a sedan, a hardtop coupe, a wagon, and a van, all powered by a highly efficient, 2.2-liter, four-cylinder engine. The Corona soon became the company's bestseller. Corona sales in the United States doubled every year for several years, with 659,189 cars sold in 1968. In the decades to follow, Toyota continued to gain market share in the US and global marketplace.

Deming's philosophy ultimately fathered the Toyota Production System, an approach to manufacturing that eventually morphed into "lean manufacturing." In 1980, Shoichiro Toyoda, honorary chairman and director of Toyota, gave Deming full credit for his country's march to dominance in the global automotive industry. "There is not a day I don't think about what Dr. Deming meant to us. Deming is the core of our management."

What did all this mean for the typical Toyota employee? For one thing, each assembly-line worker shouldered responsibility for quality and could actually stop the assembly line if he saw a mistake. Unlike the workers in American plants, who went through the motions dictated by their job descriptions, Toyota workers relentlessly looked for ways to do it right, then do it better. They brought a very different mental map to their roles on the assembly line and a deeply embedded quality pattern began to emerge (Figure 6.3).

The combination of higher quality and lower cost products boosted international demand for Japanese exports. Deming's influence ultimately helped shift the balance of economic power from the United States and Western Europe toward Asia. Without Dr. Deming's introduction of Total Quality Management, Japan might never have recovered from the devastation of World War II and gone on to become the third-largest economy in the world.

This brings us to another American who led a major transformation in the automobile industry. Mary Barra rose to the position of CEO at General Motors in January 2014. In a few short years, she orchestrated an incredible turnaround in GM's once sagging fortunes, bringing it back from the lowest

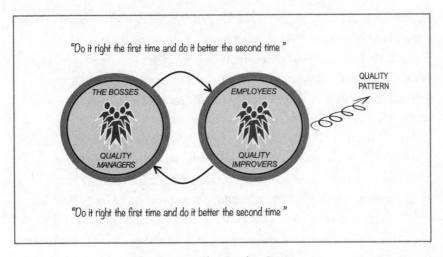

Figure 6.3. The Quality Pattern

point in her company's history—its 2009 filing for corporate bankruptcy. Barra joined GM at the age of eighteen, beginning her career inspecting fender and hood panels on the factory floor while pursuing an engineering degree at General Motors Institute (now Kettering University). Later, she completed an MBA at Stanford University. She steadily rose through the ranks at GM to positions as the head of manufacturing, engineering, human resources, and product development.

In 2014, this little-known engineer found herself in the hot glare of the media spotlight when she became the first female CEO of a large automaker. She faced a tsunami of criticism in her early days at the helm when, two months after she took charge, GM recalled 2.5 million cars plagued with faulty ignition switches. Company engineers had known about the faulty ignition for at least a decade but had failed to act, a mistake that resulted in forty-five deaths and many more injuries. To her credit, Barra did not duck responsibility for the calamity but publicly apologized and issued a blank check to compensate victims. Barra held the whole company accountable as well. No longer would she allow GM's people to conform to the old pattern of "hiding bad news." From this day forward, she expected that each and every employee would react to problems with complete openness and transparency.

The new pattern didn't just apply to manufacturing issues, it also governed the company's response to restoring its flagging fortunes in the aftermath of its 2009 bankruptcy. Barra ruthlessly ran the numbers to identify which parts of the business were making or losing money. She examined both growing and shrinking global markets. Her due diligence opened the eyes of once-complacent GM executives, who could now see the company's less profitable ventures in Russia, Australia, India, and South Africa as well its unsustainable and massive European operation.

Barra exited the Russian market, closed Chevrolet operations in Europe, shut down Holden production in Australia, and sold the European Opel/ Vauxhall unit to the Peugeot parent, PSA. She redirected the firm's focus onto the more profitable American and Chinese markets. Under Barra's leadership, GM went on to become a consistently profitable operation.

Barra's approach to manufacturing and financial problems signalled the tenets of the new culture she wanted to install at GM. For example, she crafted this encapsulation of a cultural belief she wanted all her people to hold: "Be Bold: I respectfully speak up, exchange feedback, and boldly share ideas without fear." With insight and courage, Barra launched an era of change at GM that transformed the company from a place where fearful people kept their eyes closed and their mouths shut to one where everyone made sure they saw and talked about any issue that threatened the company's success. The new mental maps, redefined roles, and the emerging pattern got results (Figure 6.4).

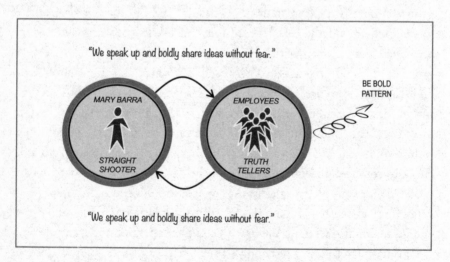

Figure 6.4. Be Bold Pattern

Henry Ford, W. Edward Deming, and Mary Barra: three examples of successful culture transformation; three strong leaders who made it happen by tackling the deeply embedded patterns that needed to change.

## TACKLING DEEPLY EMBEDDED PATTERNS

When ANZ's John McFarlane got fed up with the blame game between the head office and branch staff (in the early 2000s), he resolved to break that pattern. Among other steps, he deployed a program called "A Day in the Life," which required staff at the head office to spend a day working at a bank branch. You can imagine how much their opinions of branch workers changed when the head office employees spent the day listening to complaints, floundering when asked simple questions, and dealing with frustrated and angry customers. The head office folk went home with aching feet and sore heads, but with a much greater understanding of the challenges that branch staff faced every day.

"A Day in the Life" sounded a wake-up call that jolted employees from headquarters into action. "How," they wondered, "can we help our branches provide superior service?" This question signaled a major change in how they perceived their roles. No longer would they think and act as distant, faceless "order givers." They would now serve as "support givers," providing HR, finance, IT, and risk services to their colleagues in the branches. It didn't take long for McFarlane to see employees in both areas working together to meet the needs of customers and score higher ratings of customer satisfaction. You saw a diagram of this new pattern in chapter 5.

McFarlane saw the pattern between the head office and the branches that had gone unheeded in the past. You might wonder how executives can fail to see these dynamics, but it happens every day in organizations. You fall into a certain pattern of relating and cannot see the problems that the pattern causes in your organization. You are blind to these dynamics and they have become "how things work around here." You go to work for Gizmo, Inc., where the people in the C-suite think of the shop floor workers as replaceable automatons. So you start thinking and acting like an automaton. If you do a good job, you get promoted to manager, bringing your automaton thinking with you, but now you wield more power. And so it goes as you travel up the corporate ladder until you reach the top, where you now possess the power to change the pattern but feel so comfortable with it you would not dream of thinking and acting any other way. The only way to change this culture is to step back and see the pattern with fresh eyes and to then galvanize people to step in to break the pattern.

Remember Ben Harkness, the BuildItPro CEO we met again at the beginning of this chapter? Ben caught up with me to debrief the meeting he'd had with his leadership team that week, where he'd given Henry Tucker feedback about the billboard. Ben admitted: "I'm having trouble with the tough performance conversations. I think I've always been trying to take up the role of Mr. Nice Guy."

"Why's that a problem?" I asked with a smile. "What has it got to do with BuildItPro's performance?"

Ben thought for a minute. "Um, maybe people see me taking up the role of happy-go-lucky boss and think I'm OK with poor performance?"

I raised an eyebrow. "And?"

"And Henry Tucker in marketing figured he could take his sweet time putting up that billboard because good old Ben wouldn't do anything but flash that Mr.-Nice-Guy grin if he didn't get it done in a timely manner."

"Yes. But before we explore that, let's put it all in its proper perspective. We're talking about patterns—it's important to always remember how patterns fit into the scheme of things. Your mental map influences your role, your role shapes your behavior, and your behaviors help co-create the patterns in the culture. You can leverage these mental maps, roles, and patterns as you change the BuildItPro culture," I explained as I drew The Culture Disruptor in my notebook for Ben (Figure 6.5). Transformational leaders work with these three key elements of culture in order to bring about change.

I then shared one of my thoughts with Ben about one of the patterns at BuildItPro. "One of the big patterns I see in a lot of companies, especially with new managers and executives, is the natural tendency to want to be liked. I call it 'The Likability Pattern.' Here's what it looks like in your case. Notice how taking up the role of Mr. Nice Guy in the culture allows your employees to step into the role of underperformers. It's easy to slip into the pattern, and it's hard to break out of it" (Figure 6.6).

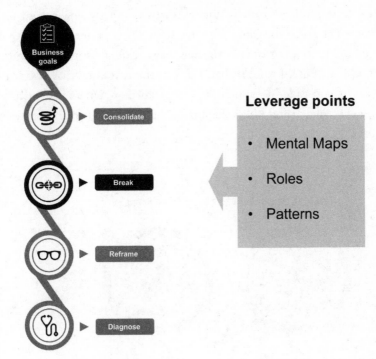

Figure 6.5. The Culture Disruptor

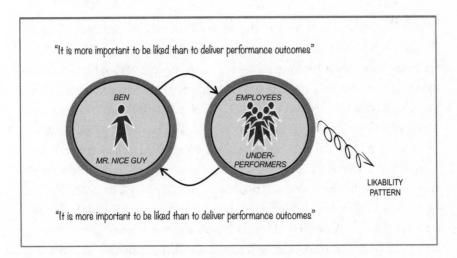

Figure 6.6. The Likability Pattern

Ben almost jumped from his chair. "Yes, that's exactly what's going on! It's high time I changed the game! Can you draw a new pattern, one that makes accountability for performance the new way of doing things in the culture?"

I nodded. "Sure. I can do that. Look at the accountability pattern that emerges if you redefine your role as a performance manager, who gives achievers feedback and holds them to account for performance outcomes" (Figure 6.7).

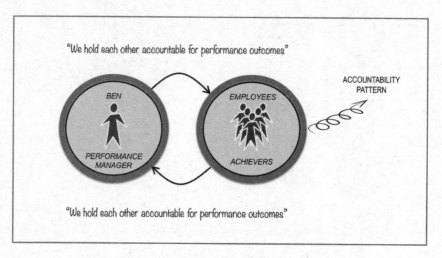

Figure 6.7. The Accountability Pattern

Ben took that insight back to the office. With his new perception of how his role cocreated a pattern he needed to break, he began to give people frank feedback about their performance. He praised people who achieved the results that the company needed and he held people to account who did not meet his performance expectations. These constructive conversations were designed to help employees get better results. This coaching proved invaluable. Many underperformers began to show measurable improvement. Those who did not accept the new ways were encouraged to find more suitable employment elsewhere. Ben was no longer Mr. Nice Guy, but instead he had stepped into the role of performance manager who gave his people the constant feedback they needed to lift their performance at work.

It took time, but it worked. Within six months, his people were actually valuing the feedback conversations about their performance, racking up significant improvements, reducing mistakes and waste, and enjoying their roles as achievers. Does this sound a little too good to be true? It's not.

*Never underestimate your power to change the culture, simply by changing your behavior.*

While culture change requires a shift in your behavior, you cannot do it alone. You need the help of a team of co-creators. In order to persuade key stakeholders to enlist in that change effort, you must create a compelling case for change.

## MAKING A COMPELLING CASE FOR CHANGE

To convince people to join a change, that may involve some personal or business risk, you must build a case for why the transformation is important to your organization. People will not join the change effort unless they have a compelling reason to do so.

In 1974, Icelandic women began a series of strikes to protest that they were getting paid 40 percent less than men for doing the same work. The women walked out of businesses and government offices and refused to cook, clean, or look after children on the protest day. The first rally, on October 24, 1974, attracted 25,000 women—an incredible number, given that the country's population was just under 220,000 at that time. The women sang protest songs, shared their stories, and listened to the speeches about the importance of their work (paid and unpaid) to society. The *Guardian* estimates that at least 90 percent of the country's women participated in the rally. Many returned home late that evening, to find exhausted husbands who had looked after the home and children for the day.

The women of Iceland have gone on strike five times since the first rally in 1974. These rallies continued to build the case for change and encouraged women to challenge the implicit agreement that "It's OK to pay men more than women." Their latest strike was in 2018, when women left work at

2:55 p.m.—to highlight the time of day that they essentially stopped earning. Despite their concerted efforts, women in Iceland were still being paid 26 percent less than their male counterparts.

These strikes have shifted public opinion and the 1974 rally triggered Iceland's equal pay law, banning gender-based wage discrimination. According to the *World Economic Forum*, in 2018, Iceland had the smallest gender pay gap (of 144 countries ranked) and was one of the most gender equal countries in the world. Icelandic women had built a compelling case for change that was summed up on the placards that women carried through the street of Reykjavik in October 1974: "When women stop, everything stops." This Icelandic case for change has inspired countless women around the world to also speak up about work inequality.

During culture transformation, the leader must employ the change skills of the Icelandic women, building a convincing case for embarking on the journey. To successfully transform workplace culture, a leader often needs to invest in new systems, processes, or training. John McFarlane at ANZ bank treated culture change as he would any other business decision, and then strove to persuade key stakeholders to get behind that investment. The business case he made repositioned the transformation as a commercial need, not just a "feel-good" culture project. The hard-nosed case for change at ANZ included the financial benefits and the tangible difference that the change would produce in terms of business outcomes.

Many leaders stall in the early days of change because they fail to treat the change as a "must-have" instead of merely a "nice-to-have" project. John McFarlane could succinctly explain why ANZ needed change, what outcomes it would produce, the logic behind making the required level of investment, and the potential risks posed by not changing. In short, he showed how the bank's very survival depended on making the change.

> *The business case moves culture change from an*
> *"optional extra" to a "must-have" undertaking.*

Let's assume you have made your case. You've rallied the team. Everyone is eager to create a better future. So, what's your plan?

## PLANNING FOR CHANGE

I always ask leaders who are beginning a culture change initiative an innocent question: "What's your plan?" I'm never surprised when that question elicits quizzical looks or blank stares. In my experience a clear plan is often the missing piece during culture transformation. Culture change falls outside the comfort zone of some managers. These bosses can prefer to focus on the problems they know how to solve, rather than on the culture issues that they actually face. Nothing will doom a change effort more quickly than the absence a well-thought out plan of action.

Take "Mark Reynolds," an executive who had taken the helm at the underperforming airline "RedJet" and was feeling terribly anxious about his first speech at the company's annual general meeting. The investors and market analysts in the room would be looking for quick solutions. How could he get them to settle down and give him time to turn things around?

He chose the path of absolute honesty. "Look, we're at the biggest turning point in RedJet's history. If we don't drastically improve our performance, we'll crash and burn. But it won't happen overnight. Let me show you a picture that represents the journey ahead of us." Mark flashed an image onto the screen: Several people standing atop a mountain, looking down on a faraway beach, a dense forest separating them from the beach. In the far distance, they could see a tiny island on the horizon. Mark spoke slowly. "We are trying to get to the Island of Better Returns, but we can't get there until we slash our way through a forest of high costs and navigate a sea of change." Mark clicked a picture of a chainsaw onto the screen: "We'll start the journey by cutting our costs to become the lowest-cost provider, turning in profits far beyond those of our industry's top performer. Then we will turn to culture change. RedJet's new culture will focus on 100 percent customer satisfaction."

Fast-forward three years. RedJet's performance had not budged an inch. Its planes almost never landed on time, customers complained about poor service, and the stock price had tumbled to a record low. What went wrong? Mark knew how to use the chainsaw, but he had failed to draw a map that would enable his people to navigate the culture change journey.

As a manager, you would not dream of constructing a factory, implementing an upgrade to your IT systems, or opening a new store without a project plan. You would probably insist on reviewing this plan in detail several times before you embarked on the project. So why do bosses tolerate a lack of planning when it comes to changing workplace culture?

The answer to this question lies in the fact that many leaders feel more confident working on the technical challenges they face every day than they do the complex issues that surround something as ambiguous and difficult to manage as culture change. If they have trained as accountants, engineers, or chemists, those roles have become an integral part of their identity at work. "You want help forecasting return on capital investment? No problem!" "You want a bridge built across that mile-wide river? Sure, I can do that!" "You want a new paint formulation that can resist the harshest weather conditions? You bet!" But ask these highly competent executives to transform the culture in their functional area, and they stare like a deer caught in the headlights of a speeding road train.

Culture is a complex, adaptive challenge, with no easy answers or ready-made solutions. It requires leaders who can plan a course of action, in the midst of uncertainty and ambiguity, because the change will not happen by itself or simply by publishing a new set of corporate values.

*Some leaders prefer to focus on the*
*problems they know how to solve,*
*rather than on the culture issues they face.*

Your culture plan examines your greatest levers for change. Should you restructure your organization to focus more intently on the customer experience? Would that require a new performance management system that measures the degree to which people take accountability for results? Does that mean you must revamp your training programs to emphasize the new values you want people to honor? What will the changes cost? How will you find the money to invest in these changes? Your own list should include the unique set of variables your plan must address. A word of caution: avoid making a long list of priorities. In my experience, you should initially focus on the top three.

*When you set too many priorities, nothing gets done.*

A good plan doesn't just describe what you will do, it tells you what you should *not* do. Good change leaders make the hard decisions and allocate scare resources to the highest priority areas. In any change effort, some people win, some lose. If your plan calls for elimination of a historical position or the cancellation of a pet project that conflicts with the tenets of the new culture, you need to prepare yourself to say no to people who rebel against the decision. Making exceptions will fuzz your focus on important steps and even detour you from the path to better results.

Once you have developed your plan you may be eager to embark on the change, but I strongly advise that you pause and test the waters before you invest all of your time and energy and dollars in the full roll-out.

## TESTING THE WATERS

John McFarlane knew that creating a better banking experience for ANZ's customers posed a mammoth challenge. He and his leadership team grappled with what changes they would need to make to create a more customer-focused culture and how that would affect the bank's thirty-two thousand employees. They decided that conducting a pilot would help answer that question. In the end, the bank would implement a company-wide project called "Restoring Customer Faith" that would restructure the bank into twenty-one business units. The restructuring, aimed at shifting accountability for meeting customer needs to local bank branches, was a huge undertaking. What if it didn't work? Knowing that it would be impossible to turn back a full rollout, the leadership team decided to carry out a pilot run in the Dandenong region of Victoria. They set it up as a mini-company based on the principles of the new culture and appointed a local CEO who would implement the culture change. Then they sat back and watched what happened. Would customer satisfaction, performance, and growth improve as much as they hoped? They did. Within four months, new accounts grew by 30 percent, customer defections plummeted by 40 percent, and employee engagement levels rose significantly. The results of this pilot gave ANZ leaders such confidence in the initiative that they voted to implement "Restoring Customer Faith" throughout the entire company.

During an ambitious culture change, you will find few, if any, ready-made, easy solutions to the problems you are trying to solve. It involves so many uncertain and ambiguous elements that it pays to conduct experiments that will show you what works and what doesn't work. I call these experiments "lighthouse projects" because, when they do work, they shine the light for everyone else who will eventually join the journey.

## · POINTS TO REMEMBER ·

- Transformational leaders break the deeply embedded patterns.
- Smart leaders study how others have done it.
- You have enormous power to change the culture, simply by changing your behavior.
- You must make a compelling case for change.
- Success depends on having a culture change plan.
- A lighthouse project can test the waters before a full roll-out.

# 7

# ENGAGE THE
# ENTIRE ORGANIZATION

### Mobilizing the
### People Who Do the Work

**Dateline: Cape Canaveral, Florida, 3:35 a.m., February 6, 2018**

Hundreds of SpaceX employees have gathered around computer consoles at the Kennedy Space Center, waiting anxiously for the test flight of the Falcon Heavy, the most powerful space rocket ever assembled. SpaceX is the brainchild of its CEO, Elon Musk, the inventor of the revolutionary Tesla automobile. He has set ambitious goals for SpaceX: reduce the cost of space flight by returning the expensive rocket's boosters to Earth, and take a major step toward his dream to colonize Mars. The rocket carries the CEO's personal midnight cherry red Tesla Roadster, with a dummy astronaut nicknamed "Starman" sitting in the driver's seat. To the underside of the sports car, workers have affixed a plaque bearing the names of every SpaceX employee who has worked on the Falcon Heavy project.

Employees hold hands as the countdown begins. At 3:45 a.m., they gasp and applaud as the Falcon Heavy lifts off in a cloud of smoke and fire. Then everyone goes silent as they await the second critical stage, the safe return of Falcon Heavy's two reusable side boosters to Earth. Several minutes pass before the boosters glide to a smooth landing on the Cape Canaveral tarmac. The room erupts in wild shouts of joy at this unprecedented accomplishment.

It took years of round-the-clock work and dedication to reach this milestone in the history of space exploration. Why did the people who worked for SpaceX engage in the endeavor? As reported in *Forbes*, former employee Josh Boehm described the working environment: "The thing is, no one, especially not Elon, is forcing you to work long hours. SpaceX just hires incredibly passionate people who love working at a rocket factory. You are your own slave driver."

Elon Musk built a passionate and high-performing culture at SpaceX that motivated talented people to reach for the stars. He did it by proclaiming an inspiring mission (on Twitter in March 2018): "Life cannot be just about solving one sad problem after another. There need to be things that inspire you, that make you glad to wake up in the morning and be part of humanity. That is why we did it. We did it for you."

Your business may not aim for the stars, but it does something that customers want and need. Whether you manufacture children's toys, play on a sports team, serve burgers at a local hangout, or build computers, you must find ways to do what Elon Musk did. In your continuing quest to break out of the old patterns, you must establish a mission that gives meaning to the work and motivates people to go above and beyond their mere job descriptions to fulfill this vision.

## MAKING THE WORK MEANINGFUL

Let's revisit Chloe Khan, the manager of the Waterworks maintenance team we met in chapter 4. You may recall that her team maintained the treatment plants and networks for Metro City, a seemingly mundane undertaking. But Chloe established the mission that made the work far from mundane. When she took over the team, Chloe found it mired in a blame game where everyone accused everyone but themselves for the problems that plagued the team's performance. She knew she needed to put a stop to that damaging cycle and get her people taking individual and team accountability for solving problems.

Chloe began the culture change at an unexpected meeting she convened with all her managers and front-line supervisors. Some members of the team, taken by surprise, marched into the canteen straight from the wastewater treatment plants, still wearing their bright yellow gear. Most sat with arms folded across their chest, waiting for the big boss to assign the blame to them for everything that was going wrong at Waterworks.

Chloe surprised them. Rather than pointing an accusing finger, she asked a simple question of a senior manager. "Randall, tell me, please, what's your job here? You know, what's your role?" Randall did not hesitate. "I'm a supervisor in charge of the wastewater treatment plant." Chloe smiled. "No. You're not. You're the guy in charge of protecting the health and well-being of an entire city." She then outlined Waterworks' history, beginning with the era when cholera and other water-borne diseases plagued the region. "We cleaned it up," she told the crew. "Without clean water, there would be no life on Earth." Chloe began her campaign to break the deeply embedded pattern of blaming others for problems by connecting people to the mission of Waterworks. Over the next nine months she reinforced the message. Those who "got it" kept their jobs and won promotions. Those who didn't looked elsewhere for work.

The psychiatrist Viktor Frankl wrote about the power of purpose in his best-selling book, *Man's Search for Meaning*. Imprisoned by the Nazis in various concentration camps during World War II, Frankl could have gone insane as he watched his pregnant wife and parents die in the camps, but he didn't. He survived because he found and followed a purpose in his life. Writing about his experiences at Auschwitz, Frankl described how he survived the horrific conditions of camp life by caring for and supporting other inmates both personally and professionally. Service to a cause even greater than the welfare of himself and his family enabled him to turn what could have been a soul-shattering experience into a record of accomplishment.

Success in life and work depends less on what you do, than on why you do it. A bricklayer can place one brick on top of another, but the one who feels a sense of purpose, that he's not just laying bricks but playing an important part in the construction of a purposeful building—whether it be a school, a home, or a place of worship—is most likely to do the most productive work.

Likewise, Apple does not just churn out digital devices. The company delivers products and features designed to enhance users' lives, products no one could have imagined ten years ago. In 2018, Apple launched a series of category-defining products that wowed the market: AirPods, tiny wireless Bluetooth headphones that users could pair with the company's many other products, including the best-selling Apple Watch Series 3; ARKit, a device that allowed game players to enjoy an augmented reality experience on their iPhones and iPads and iMacs; iPhoneX, with facial recognition, high-resolution screen, and improved camera quality; and HomePod, a wireless smart speaker users could operate by telling their digital assistant Siri to switch on the smart TV, turn up the heat, or dim the lights.

This suite of category-defining products helped make Apple the first company to achieve a valuation of one trillion dollars. CEO Tim Cook said this about Apple's performance (as reported in *Fast Company*): "You could walk down this aisle (at Apple) and talk to ten people, and they'd be totally different, but we all have the same common purpose. . . . Our North Star is making the best products in the world. That's the thing that joins us all together." Little wonder Apple won the number one spot on the *Forbes* list of the World's Most Innovative Companies in 2018.

Purpose. Like *culture*, it's a simple but elusive word. No matter how you define it, however, it's the fuel that drives every successful company's performance engine. My agent Michael Snell found it in the world of college textbook publishing when his mentor Jim Leisy asked him to describe what book publishers do. Michael replied, "We publish books." Leisy disagreed. "No, we don't. We package information that can change people's lives. That physics text we will publish next year may set the next Albert Einstein on the path to breakthrough ideas." Everyone who works for a living wants to do something meaningful that might enhance the lives of others. It's a basic human desire. Sure, you want to make money, but as Jim Leisy went on to tell my agent Michael, "Money is just the yardstick we use to measure whether or not we are touching people's lives. Do meaningful work and the money will follow."

Success depends on purpose and meaning, but it also depends on the right people doing the right work at the right time.

## CHOOSING THE RIGHT PEOPLE

The people in your organization make all the difference in the world. But they need to align wth your culture. Zappos, the billion-dollar online shoe and clothing retailer (now owned by Amazon), built one of the most talked-about cultures in the world. The CEO, Tony Hsieh, applied a deceptively simple test whenever a shuttle bus picked up job candidates at the airport. After the shuttle delivered folks to headquarters, Hsieh questioned the driver about his passengers' behavior. "Were they kind and appreciative or aloof and insensitive?" Were they, in a word, respectful? Nice people get hired. Rude people look for work elsewhere. As Hsieh explained in a speech at the 2013 START Conference, "We've actually passed on a lot of really smart, talented people whom we know can make an immediate impact on our top or bottom line, but if they're not good for the company culture, we won't hire them for that reason alone."

However, the ultimate test of culture fit at Zappos happens one week after a new recruit has joined the firm and is still in the midst of training. The company offers the new hire a $4,000 check to leave the company and never come back. Does that sound absurd? Perhaps. The test is aimed at assessing a new employee's commitment to the job. Do a lot of people take the money and run? No, an impressive 97 percent opt to stay with the company. Interestingly, Zappos features regularly on *Fortune*'s "Top 100 companies to work for" list.

Leaders in great cultures focus on hiring the right people for the job. The Ritz-Carlton hotel chain, renowned for service above and beyond first class, made sure it hired people who could bring the hotel's famous service promise to life. While managers carefully trained people in the technical aspects of the job, they worried far more about honing their relationship skills. Competitors might try to match the quality of Ritz-Carlton's rooms and decor, but they could not easily replicate the hotel staff's impeccable service. They believed in hiring people with innate relationship skills and helping them refine those skills, a tactic that left their competitors struggling to keep up.

*In successful cultures, leaders hire people*
*who will bring the desired culture to life.*

Leaders in great cultures work relentlessly to find the right talent for their team. They also weed out those who don't buy into the culture's values and who fail to demonstrate them in everything they do. It may seem a little harsh, but great leaders are prepared to let talented people go, if they do not meet the culture expectations.

That doesn't mean that the right people always have the answers. No, the right people solve the right problems at the right time.

## TURNING EVERYONE INTO A PROBLEM SOLVER

Leaders in high-performing cultures realize that they don't have all the answers. When problems emerge (and they always do), they rely on their people to come up with the best solutions. It turns out that the most creative and often surprising solutions come from those who do the work. The drone manufacturer DJI, based in Shenzhen (China's Silicon Valley), offers a terrific example. Founded by Frank Wang in his Hong Kong university dorm in 2006, DJI was worth $10 billion in 2018, and its drone sales have (at least) tripled every year between 2009 to 2014 (according to *Seeking Alpha*). DJI achieved this growth by solving the troublesome problems that plagued the industry, turning once clunky, unreliable flying machines into sleek and efficient human helpers.

For instance, in May 2017 DJI launched Spark, the tiniest drone available at the time. At just $499, this pocket-sized drone offered astonishing capabilities, including object tracking, obstacle avoidance, and computer-generated vision. You wanted to capture a bird's-eye view of your family playing its traditional multigenerational football game at the local park? Just launch your sky cam, perform a few simple hand gestures, and voila, you have captured a priceless memento your children can show to their children.

Did some Einstein-level engineer come up with this handy product? No. It came about as the result of DJI's reliance on its people's ability to solve even the most challenging problems. More than 25 percent of the company's eleven thousand employees share accountability for R&D. As Wang observed, "We do this through an unparalleled commitment to R&D, a culture of constant innovation and curiosity, and a focus on transforming complex technology into easy-to use devices." As a result, DJI came to dominate the global drone market with a 70 percent market share. In a marketing coup, it won an Emmy in 2017 for its sweeping aerial footage in such television shows as *Game of Thrones* and *The Amazing Race*. Little wonder DJI made it to the number 35 spot on the 2018 list of *Fortune*'s Most Innovative Companies.

*A problem-solving culture inspires people to come up with wildly successful solutions.*

The American giants Google and Amazon took this advice to heart, assigning the role of "innovator" to every single employee. In Google's case, the company topped the Boston Consulting Group's list of the fifty most innovative companies in 2018 with a track record of unparalleled trailblazing services such as Maps, Search, Gmail, and YouTube. How did such innovation come about? Google's chairman, Eric Schmidt, put it succinctly on the company's website. "You have to have the culture and you need to get it right."

Google cascaded problem-solving to every level of its organization with the concept "10x thinking," which encouraged employees to improve what Google offered its customers tenfold rather than the mere 10 percent that would satisfy most companies. Google also adhered to its famous "20 percent" rule, giving employees one day per week to work on intractable problems. Many of the company's greatest innovations have come from this day of innovation, including Google News, Gmail, and AdSense. Google Suggest was the brainchild of engineer Kevin Gibbs who, in 2004, used his day of innovation to dream up an addition to Google's Search function that offers suggestions for your search as you type in a topic. Users often wonder how Google Search can read their minds. Of his breakthrough idea Gibbs said, "We've found that Google Suggest not only makes it easier to type in your favorite searches but also gives you a playground to explore what others are searching and learn about things you haven't dreamt of."

Dreams also come true at Amazon, recognized as one of the world's most innovative companies. Amazon's cofounder and guiding thinker, Jeff

Bezos, deliberately harnessed the problem-solving power of his company's employees to come up with cutting-edge solutions. People. That's how Amazon joined the trillion-dollar club. Since its launch in 1995, Amazon went on to become to the world's biggest online retailer, selling everything from A to Z. "You need an aardvark? We've got it. You want a zebra? Just click your mouse."

Bezos believes that every Amazonian should think like an owner of the business. In an interview with CNBC, Bezos described how he encourages his people to "look around corners to serve the customer" and not to take shortcuts. The Bezos mantra, "It's still day one," rings in employees' ears every day, reminding them that tomorrow they can create something that no one has dreamed possible before.

At Amazon, it's not just a mantra that ignites innovative thinking. The company installed a system to make it happen. You just came up with a cool idea? First, you write "The Press Release," an internal document that captures the idea in marketing terms. For example, The Press Release for Prime and Prime Now (Amazon's fast same-day delivery service) promised significant benefits to the customer. Next you write "The Six-Pager," which makes a compelling business case for the product or service, articulating the commercial opportunity in the marketplace and providing the hard data that supports it. You list everything from required capital investment to supply chain and logistics needs. A business owner would do the same. Amazon's employees (thinking like business owners) have created one of the fastest growing companies in the world, with year-over-year revenue growth of 31 percent from 2006 to 2018, (according to *Statistica*), and have cemented the company's position as the go-to shopping destination for 75 percent of the US population that shops online.

This may sound fairly straightforward, but it can take time and hard work to create a problem-solving culture. As you guide people on the journey from the old way of expecting someone else to solve problems to owning the problem and solving it yourself, you must nudge people out of their comfort zones, replacing their old mental maps and roles with new ones. That takes more than good intentions and well-crafted values statements.

Suppose you manage a production line that churns out a hundred widgets an hour. Over the years, you have come to accept a certain amount of waste, say 15 percent. When the company's CEO decides that for competitive and financial reasons the company needs to reduce waste to 5 percent, do you sit around waiting for your boss to do it for you? That's probably not the best approach. Do you do it yourself? That might be the quickest solution. Or do you ask Sally and Ted, who have been running the widget machine for the past three years to chop out that 10 percent of waste? You guessed it. The best solutions always come from the people closest to the work. When overseeing a change effort, smart leaders loosen the reins and relinquish control of the problem-solving process, inspiring their people to find the most effective and creative solutions. Sally surprises everybody when she comes to work one morning and inserts an ordinary stainless-steel paper clip in the widget machine's innards. Voilà, less conveyor belt wiggle, 10 percent less waste.

Leaders who push people to change or threaten them by saying, "You must do this, or else!" find that the harder they push, the harder their people push back, often in subtle ways that end up sabotaging the cause. It's far better to create an environment that gives people the freedom to solve problems. If you inspire Sally and Ted to find a way to get a better result and reward them when they do find it, it becomes their widget machine. Feeling a sense of ownership, they buy into solving the problem themselves. Imagine the results if your whole team thought and acted that way.

## KEEPING THE TEAM'S EYES ON THE PRIZE

In chapter 6 we saw how the women of Iceland made such a compelling case for wage equality, that their message reached people in every town and village across the country—resulting in a 90 percent turnout (of the total female working population) at the Reykjavik rally in 1974. Inspirational leaders know how to galvanize groups of people and direct them toward the change goals. Take Spotify, the music-streaming company based in Sweden that has revolutionized the music industry. Spotify, founded in 2008 by Daniel Ek and Martin Lorentzon, made $4.6 billion in 2018 (a 40 percent increase over the previous year). An unusual business model sets Spotify apart from its rivals. When the company plans to introduce a new product, perhaps a new music player, it bands together a team of about forty people to put their collective minds and energy into the endeavor. These teams, in turn, consist of smaller ten-to-twelve person groups called "squads," each devoted to a particular aspect of the ultimate customer experience. The teams function like mini startups in which senior leadership invests valuable corporate resources. Operating with complete freedom and autonomy, these dedicated teams get amazing results.

For instance, Spotify offers its customers the opportunity to create data-powered personal playlists that reflect a particular mood or genre. If Trish wants to listen to classic Christmas carols while wrapping presents for her loved ones, she simply asks the system to play Bing Crosby's "White Christmas," and in an instant Spotify's sophisticated data algorithms produce an almost infinite supply of songs that fit the same festive season bill. According to *Fast Company*, one Spotify product, Discover Weekly ("a playlist made just for you, based on your music tastes, every Monday"), provided 5 billion tunes to over 40 million people in less than a year, more than Apple Music and Tidal combined. Despite tough competition from heavyweights like Apple and Amazon, in 2018 Spotify boasted over 180 million active users and over 83 million paid subscribers (35 million in North America alone). The company's teams helped make that happen.

A sense of belonging can help to create a high performing culture, where people give their discretionary effort to the achievement of the team's goals. Garry Ridge, the CEO of WD-40 Company, knew how to do that. WD-40, a San Diego–based manufacturer of household chemicals, generated revenues of $380 million in 2018, selling its products in over 176 countries around the world. Ridge tells a story about his first job as a newspaper boy in the Sydney suburb of Five Dock. On his daily rounds he enjoyed meeting an elderly woman, Mrs. Peel, and she looked forward to his visits, greeting him every day with a bag of candy. It was Garry's first experience of discretionary effort inspired by really caring about someone. And in return Mrs. Peel made him feel cared about as well.

Fast forward to today and Ridge is now CEO of WD-40 but has not forgotten Mrs. Peel or the impact this connection made on him. He has created a highly successful company by building a culture where people feel safe, supported, and appreciated. So much so that 99 percent of employees answered 'yes' to a question in the company's 2018 employee engagement survey: "*I love to tell people that I work for WD-40 Company.*"

In an interview with Ridge, he spoke to me about how he strives to create a "tribal culture" at WD-40. "Tribe is about belonging and contributing to the whole—not individually winning and losing at all costs." So how has this culture of belonging impacted the financial results at WD-40? Over the past twenty years, sales quadrupled, market valuation went from $250 million to $2.5 billion, and total shareholder return hovered at 15 percent each year. Ridge says this about his company's success: "Engagement, and thus personal investment in the organization, stems from positive experiences within the tribe, which yields the applause of financial performance."

Every business must perform financially or go into decline. Outper-formance does not happen by accident. It happens when people strive for goals that may at first seem beyond their grasp. Effective leaders set challeng-ing goals that will require everyone's utmost effort and creativity. Soccer coaches know all about that. I saw it firsthand when I decided to shadow the Sheffield United Football Club, to see how high performers operate. A bud-ding organizational psychologist, I wanted to know what it takes for individ-uals and teams to stay at the top of their game. Over the course of the season, I witnessed a powerful culture motivate players to stretch their minds and bodies to the limit. Every minute of every practice and every game the players set their sights on winning the Football Association Cup Final, a goal only one team will achieve each season. That objective was the focal point of the team. Players shared stories about how they reminded themselves of this su-preme goal with stickers plastered on bathroom mirrors, signs tacked to bed-room ceilings, and magnets stuck onto refrigerator doors. These reminders spurred them to do their best, crawling out of bed at the crack of dawn each morning to throw themselves into a grueling training regime that taxed even the fittest players. Yes, they brought a certain amount of raw talent to the game, but a challenging goal inspired them to sharpen that talent and put every ounce of their effort into the game.

We all need targets in our work. They help us to gauge how we are tracking in the achievement of our goals. The more concrete these goals can be, the better. The Results Converted (Figure 7.1) shows you how you can translate abstract wishes into concrete objectives. So "best in class performance" might become, "achieve a 25 percent increase in net profit." The vague goal of "new product innovation" might shift to "reach $14 million revenue for the new X Factor product." An ambition to "delight customers'" might be replaced by, "ensure 95 percent of customers are extremely satisfied." Finally, instead of wishing to be "the best football team," the Sheffield United Football Club might focus instead on "winning the FA Cup."

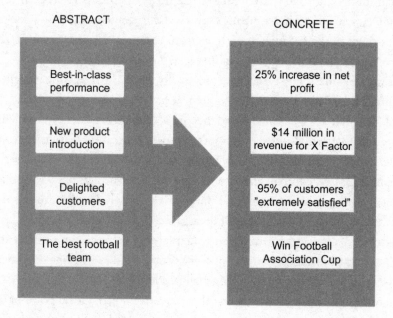

Figure 7.1. The Results Converter

Try setting your own concrete goals to create a focused and higher performing team.

As the ancient proverb holds, every thousand-mile journey begins with a single step. Since the whole journey may take a few million steps, you need to give people feedback about their progress along the way.

## MASTERING THE ART OF CONSTRUCTIVE FEEDBACK

Feedback helps people see their progress (or lack thereof) as they move toward their team's or their organization's goals. It reinforces their will and provides guidance on why they should break out of the old habits to improve their performance. Great change leaders offer frequent positive, appreciative, and constructive feedback that nudges the culture toward the desired future state. Netflix does it by encouraging people to give timely, helpful, and honest feedback to their colleagues. As the company's website declares, "Say what you think, when it's in the best interest of Netflix, even when it's uncomfortable."

The leaders at Netflix believe in making feedback an integral part of working life. In place of conventional performance reviews, managers give their people honest, continuous feedback in an effort to build what Netflix calls the "Dream Team." They want every person to strive for extraordinary performance every minute of every day. Senior executives ask managers to apply what they call the "Keeper Test." In essence, "What would you do if one of your people is thinking about leaving the team? Would you try to persuade them to stay, or would you encourage them to find a better fit somewhere else?" If a manager would try hard to keep an employee from exiting, that employee is a keeper. If not, it's time to look for a potential star to fill that position. Underperformers receive a generous severance package; stars continue to shine. With respect to feedback, Netflix CEO Reed Hastings once said, "In the tension between honesty and kindness, we lean into honesty." The financial results prove the wisdom of this approach. Netflix gross revenues grew from $11 billion in 2017 to $15 billion in 2018.

Constant constructive feedback helps employees assess their progress as they strive to achieve the change goals. Employees at Bridgewater Associates, one of the largest hedge funds in the world, manage $160 billion in investment money with what the company calls a culture of "radical transparency." Ray Dalio, who founded the company in his two-bedroom New York apartment in 1975, wanted to create a workplace where employees could exchange controversial ideas without fear of ridicule or punishment. If you work for Dalio, you must learn to tell the "radical truth" and respond honestly to every idea you hear, no matter how outrageous or outlandish. This approach does not work for a lot of people—30 percent of employees leave within their first two years. Those who stay turn in great results, with Bridgewater topping the 2017 list of the biggest hedge fund moneymakers ever, delivering $50 billion to its clients since the company's inception.

While brutally frank honesty works for Bridgewater Associates, Southwest Airlines uses a kinder, gentler approach to feedback that contributed greatly to the company's extraordinarily high level of employee engagement. Southwest's former CEO, Herb Kelleher, used feedback to sustain a work environment where staff were encouraged to bring their whole authentic selves to work. You may have seen the viral YouTube video in which an employee delivers a rap version of the company's safety announcement. At Southwest, you can bring your talent to work, whether it's a knack for rhyming or an offbeat sense of humor. More important, if you did something noteworthy to delight customers, you received one of Kelleher's coveted "shout-outs." He let pilots, flight attendants, and cleaners know that he personally valued their contribution. If you award folks a few dollars for doing something wonderful, the money will disappear in a flash; if you give them a generous dose of public appreciation, the praise is likely to have a more lasting impact. This principle helped fuel Southwest's best-in-class on-time departure record. Today, under the stewardship of CEO Gary C. Kelly, the company was named the best US carrier by Trip Advisor (in 2018), in large part because its people love their jobs and remain fiercely loyal to the company. According to *Forbes*, voluntary turnover at Southwest hovers around 2 percent, a low number that would delight any human resources director.

When successful change leaders catch people doing terrific work to achieve the company's goals, they shine a spotlight on those achievements. Early achievers become role models for others. When someone in your organization displays highly prized cultural traits, turn that person into a beacon for others to follow. When Ted sees Sally receieve accolades (and a nice bonus) for her waste-saving gizmo, he will likely look for ways to win the same sort of praise (and cash reward) for his own creative solution.

Good teachers get results with reinforcement. Good students enjoy the learning that comes with constructive feedback. Whatever the cultural traits you want your people to learn and apply in their work, reward them when they perform well, and give them appreciative guidance when they fall short of the mark. The leaders at the Ritz-Carlton Hotel Company reinforced the new ways they wanted their people to behave by developing an organizational "mantra" that summed up the hotel chain's service philosophy: "We are ladies and gentlemen, serving ladies and gentlemen." While this simple statement describes the role employees should play in delivering great service to customers, Ritz-Carlton's CEO, Herve Humler, knew that words alone would not create a world-class, customer-focused culture. To reinforce the behaviors that would accomplish that goal, he instigated fifteen-minute stand-up meetings that became known as the "daily lineup." During these brief, focused get-togethers, team members shared their experiences and received praise for anything that helped bring the desired service culture to life. Feedback need not come solely from above; it can come from the folks with whom you work shoulder-to-shoulder every day. Whatever its source, it reinforces the way people think about and perform their work.

In great organizations the leaders understand that the culture is shaped in every single interaction. They reinforce the new expectations, monitor the standards, and give regular feedback to employees about how they are tracking. In high performing cultures the leaders realize that they have to do more than simply publish the expectations, if they are to see change to happen.

*Successful change leaders move beyond the slogans to bring the culture to life every day at work.*

Effective leaders create the culture in their daily interactions and behaviors. They reinforce the new ways and embed the emerging practices. These bosses realize that culture does not arise from slogans, mantras, or values statements assembled by the HR department. They employ daily routines to remind people about what matters and they reinforce the desired culture at every opportunity. In the next chapter we will examine how you can also reinforce the new patterns by aligning your organization's processes, policies, and procedures to the aspirational culture.

•   •   •

## · POINTS TO REMEMBER ·

- Great culture leaders make the work meaningful.
- Alignment with the desired culture, not just technical skills, is essential when hiring people.
- Change accelerates when people take up their problem-solving role.
- Challenging goals can keep people focused on what matters most.
- Feedback can reinforce the desired culture.
- Constructive feedback can help people break out of the old patterns.

# 8

## ALIGN PROCESSES, POLICIES, AND PROCEDURES

### Designing New Work Systems and Spaces

On a brisk Monday evening in October, Sam Goldman prepares her living room for a football party, surrounding her big flat-screen television with comfortable sofas and a broad coffee table. She can't wait for her beloved New England Patriots to crush their archrivals, the Green Bay Packers. The doorbell rings. Her best friends, Tyrone and Ava, arrive, open a bottle of white wine and declare, "Hey, we're starving!"

Sam grabs her smartphone and, with a few quick taps, accesses Domino's mobile app and orders two large everything-but-the-anchovies pizzas. A few minutes later, she checks her order status and announces: Excellent! Jack, the pizza guy, is already making our order! She shows Tyrone the Domino's Pizza Tracker on her phone. They watch the delivery car winding through the Back Bay streets until, presto, the doorbell rings again. "Watch out, they're hot!" warns Sam as the three friends tuck into their food and watch the Patriots' return specialist run the kickoff back for a touchdown.

What a world! You can order your Domino's pizza with a call, a text, a tweet, or a post on Facebook Messenger. Type the order on your smart watch or tablet, or click your device to ask Dom, Alexa, Echo, or Google Home to fill it. The skeptics ask: "Why do you need all this technology? Don't customers prefer dealing with real, live people?" Perhaps many do, but, as chief digital officer Dennis Maloney said about the company's innovative experiment, "We make sure that everything we put out there creates a great or better experience for the Domino's fan when it comes to ordering, getting, or enjoying Domino's pizza." The company even tried drone delivery in New Zealand and put driverless cars on the streets of Ann Arbor, Michigan, in an effort to create an even more exciting customer experience.

Whatever the future of this sort of experiment (delivery by drones?), Domino's customer-driven initiatives generated tremendous public relations stories in the media and produced business results for the company. In 2017, President and CEO Patrick Doyle achieved his goal of becoming the top pizza company in the world, edging out longtime rival Pizza Hut, with more than $12 billion in global sales (according to CNBC).

Businesses have always relied on systems and processes and policies and procedures that enable their people to satisfy customers and deliver business results. New technology makes it possible to do it bigger, faster, and smarter. Companies that get it right lock in greater customer loyalty. Staying at the forefront of technology helped build industry leader Domino's innovative culture that gets results. In 2018, 60 percent of the company's sales came through digital channels (according to *Bloomberg*) because the new generation of customers loved the convenience of ordering their food with a simple, "Hey, Alexa, order two pepperoni pizzas from Domino's."

Culture is a people thing, but it's also a process thing. During the third step on The Culture Disruptor (*Break* the patterns) you can leverage process and system changes to create the desired culture. Aligning your processes, procedures, policies, and physical environment to your change goals, can strongly reinforce the aspirational culture. Changes to these systems and spaces can help you continue on your journey to break the old patterns. Whatever new and disruptive technologies emerge in the future, smart leaders will always need to pay attention to what I call the five key system levers during culture change: Digital Technology, Performance and Reward Sys-

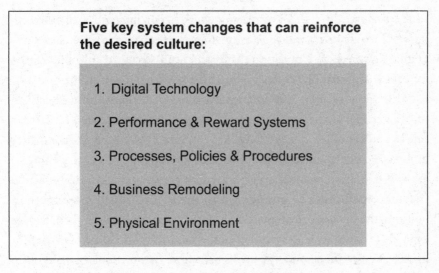

**Five key system changes that can reinforce the desired culture:**

1. Digital Technology

2. Performance & Reward Systems

3. Processes, Policies & Procedures

4. Business Remodeling

5. Physical Environment

Figure 8.1. Five Key System Reinforcers

tems, Processes, Policies, and Procedures, Business Remodeling, and the Physical Environment (Figure 8.1).

System changes can reinforce your desired culture, but only if you simultaneously shift the underlying patterns—otherwise people are likely to work around the new systems to go back to the old ways of doing things. Let's start by examining how digital technology can accelerate culture transformation.

## EMBRACING THE DIGITAL FUTURE

There's one key reason why leaders embark on culture change: to get better results. In business, often it comes down to more effectively and efficiently connecting with customers, providing ever more convenient and delightful customer experiences, and forging undying customer loyalty. Even a coffee-maker does it. Technology has been advancing at such mind-bending speed, these examples will be outdated before you turn this page. I'd like to offer a few examples from ancient history, all the way back to 2018. That year, Starbucks, one of the best-known companies in the world, operated more than twenty-eight thousand stores globally. It didn't do that by making the best coffee in the world; it did it by placing a huge bet on integrating digital technology into its brick-and-mortar in-store experience, with the company's Digital Flywheel, an innovation that dramatically changed customer behavior patterns by enabling coffee enthusiasts to order and pay online.

Starbucks cemented customer loyalty through a combination of user rewards, a personalized app, easy payments, and online ordering. By 2018, a full 18 percent of Starbucks' 75 million customers were using the company's mobile app to generate 36 percent of the company's sales (according to TechHQ). Starbucks could even personalize the app to help boost sales and encourage customers to buy additional items. This added more revenue, boosting the percentage of user purchases of overall sales, with their average expenditures growing at 8 percent per annum (double the growth rate for in-store sales). The company's investment in digital technology paid off in increased sales and more delighted customers. President and CEO Kevin Johnson explained the 2017 results ($22 billion, up 5 percent from the previous year): "Establishing digital relationships with many more customers represents a significant growth opportunity, as we have proven that a direct communications channel combined with personalization enhances the customer experience and drives customer engagement."

It may seem like an obvious and easily implemented decision now, but adaptation to the digital world requires overhauling substantial parts of the organization, no mean feat for a company as big as Starbucks. You can expand the problem exponentially for a sprawling organization like Walmart, the largest retailer on the planet. Needing to compete more effectively with Amazon, the traditional brick-and-mortar retailer got off to a slow start with its digital transformation but eventually reaped huge benefits from the program. In 2011, Walmart set up its Online Retailing Unit. By 2015, the unit was employing 3,600 people and spending $1 billion per annum on creating better experiences for device-happy customers.

It may sound easy after the fact, but digital transformation is tough, especially if it involves overhauling a multinational corporation, like Walmart. The traditional bricks-and-mortar retailer embraced digital technology after a delayed start against Amazon. In a push to become a retailer of choice, Walmart took some big strides into the digital world, modifying its old business model, linking e-commerce to its real-world stores, and making it easier for customers to look for products, check prices, and make purchases. The steps included a Data Café, a mobile app, online ordering, and digital maps for use on smartphones that allowed customers to locate items in the store. Workers, armed with new apps on their mobile devices, could manage routine tasks, freeing them to serve customers. If you were a busy and impatient customer, you could ask a staff member to settle your bill with Walmart Pay, a digital payment platform that accelerated the checkout process. Along the way, you might take advantage of the app's Savings Catcher, a popular price-matching tool that promised customers they could trust Walmart prices. Each of these customer-oriented offerings help make the Walmart culture become even more customer-centric. Wanda Young, vice president of media and digital marketing, said in a speech at the SM2 conference, "Those who have the app are making twice as many trips to Walmart, and their spend is 40 percent more." The retail giant was seeing the tangible benefits of its investment in digital technology.

According to CapGemini, between 2011 and 2014, Walmart's online sales grew by 150 percent, from $4.9 billion to $12.2 billion, making it America's second largest online retailer. In 2018, Walmart's omnichannel strategy delivered the company's strongest sales gain in more than a decade. Walmart's leaders expected to achieve more revenue gains by expanding home delivery to reach 40 percent of the US population by the end of 2018. From top to bottom, Walmart was making great strides toward breaking out of the old ways and creating a more customer-focused culture. As President and CEO Doug McMillon explained, "We are moving with speed to become more of a digital enterprise and better serve customers."

Bank of America (BoA) was also moving to create a more customer-focused culture, by implementing digital technology. In 2018, BoA's CEO, Brian Moynihan, introduced Erica, a new virtual chat bot, to the bank's 25 million mobile users. With Erica's assistance, users could access banking with voice or text commands and check balances, transfer money between accounts, or search past transactions. Erica could accumulate customer information, analyze spending patterns, and provide guidance on making better financial decisions. Digital technology required significant investment and, in 2018 alone, the bank spent $2.7 billion on technology enhancements. According to Michelle Moore, head of BoA's digital banking, "Everything we do is based on what we hear from our clients: how they want to interact with us, and how we can make their financial lives better."

Applications like Erica enable organizations to engage more deeply with customers, especially the much-sought-after eighteen-to-thirty-four-year-old demographic. According to Bankrate, 64 percent of millennials surveyed in 2018 said they had at least one full-service banking app on their phone. BoA wanted to exploit that fact by making Erica not only a digital bank teller but also a trusted financial advisor. Trust. Nothing builds stronger bonds of customer loyalty. In the case of BoA, Erica played a major role in accomplishing that with more than 1 million customers using Erica within two months of launch.

Who knows what new devices will come along in the future, but whether they spring from the world of artificial intelligence (think devices with facial recognition), from the imagination of an engineering prodigy at Harvard (think Facebook), or the collective effort of private and public organizations (think moon landing), they will all require companies to create the sort of culture that can break out of the old patterns to take full advantage of these digital solutions in the marketplace.

No matter what technologies you adopt to serve your customers more quickly, it won't happen without the human touch. You think Amazon is a pure technology and e-commerce enterprise? Think again. The company's leaders know the importance of person-to-person contact. That's why Amazon opened its first "four-star" store in New York, in September 2018. The store sells toys, books, devices, gifts, and school supplies that have won four-star customer ratings. The sales staff is technologically savvy. Behind the scenes, Amazon's digital employees try hard to be people-savvy. Amazon's chief financial officer, Brian T. Olsavsky, told investors in 2017, "The stores represent another way to reach the customer and to test what resonates with them." This sort of thinking led to Amazon acquiring the Whole Foods grocery chain (in 2017) with its 450 brick-and-mortar stores.

Walmart executives also keep people in the picture. They adopted digital technology in order to improve the in-store experience for shoppers. Customers could order online, then pick up their goods at the local store, using express lanes. "Scan and Go" allowed customers to scan items on their smartphones as they shopped and avoid long checkout lines. About its digital presence, CEO Doug McMillon said (in his August 2018 report to the market), "We're pleased with how customers are responding to the way we're leveraging stores and e-commerce to make shopping faster and more convenient."

So, you're the CEO of Granny Jane's Mincemeat Pies. You want to go digital. Do you fire all of your older pie makers and replace them with fresh-faced tech-smart kids? Do you throw out your old-fashioned customer care department and install a bunch of fancy tinny-voiced robots? No, you don't. Yes, you may need to hire new people with new skills in the new age of digital everything, but you can also bring your veterans up to speed. Give the newcomers and the veterans the chance to learn from each other. And, yes, you may need to automate a lot of functions, but you must never lose sight of the value of the human touch, even in this world of rapidly evolving technology.

Remember that culture is "how (*people* make) things work around here." Machines can do a lot of things, but they cannot (and I bet they never will) fully duplicate what people can do: apply common sense, dream up new concepts, develop keen self-awareness, connect seemingly unrelated dots, invent the better mousetrap, and feel true love and compassion. People need people. They also need recognition and rewards for a job well done.

## FINE-TUNING PERFORMANCE AND REWARD SYSTEMS

The 2008 collapse of Lehman Brothers, the fourth-largest US investment bank at that time, almost brought down the global financial system and broke the record for the largest bankruptcy in US history. The collapse sent world banking systems into panic as the subprime lending bubble burst. American housing prices fell by 31.8 percent, millions of people lost their jobs, another 800,000 lost their homes to foreclosure, and the world's major economies suffered their deepest recessions since the Great Depression of the 1930s. In the wake of the crisis, the spotlight shone on the flood of mortgages that banks gave to subprime borrowers, people with poor credit histories, all across America. Public outrage targeted bankers who doled out these loans, that even a financial dolt could see that the borrowers could not afford to repay. The public expressed even more anger over the massive bonuses the banks awarded the employees who lent the money. As the accounting firm PricewaterhouseCoopers declared in a study titled "Pay: What

Motivates Financial Services Executives? The Psychology of Incentives": "The banking crisis was, in part, caused by excessive short-term risk-taking encouraged by a bonus culture" (August 2012). Despite huge taxpayer-financed bailouts governments used to shore up the finance industry, two years after the recession ended, US unemployment rates still hovered above 9 percent.

The performance and reward system in an organization can create a culture for good or for greed. These systems send powerful signals to employees about what the organization values and what rewards they can expect to receive if they honor those values. For example, Facebook's leaders, wishing to create an open and transparent culture, designed the company's performance and pay system to reflect this intent. Managers and employees went through a biannual review process, which directly linked pay to performance ratings. It occurred out in the open, not behind closed doors. The process included both a self-evaluation and colleagues' opinions. To minimize overly positive or negative ratings, those implementing the system compared various people's ratings for consistency. Facebook's Vice President of People Lori Goler told *Inc.com*, "Openness and transparency, building community, collaborating—it's all part of the way we work together." The job-rating site Glassdoor has (more than once) named Facebook as one of the best places to work in the United States.

More and more companies are redesigning the way they reward performance. At Accenture, the $39 billion professional services firm, leaders threw out the traditional approach to performance management when they discovered that 75 percent of the annual review process involved talking *about* the company's 330,000 employees and only 25 percent of the time involved talking *to* them. Pierre Nanterme (CEO, 2011–2019) and Ellyn Shook (chief human resources officer) doubted the effectiveness of that approach. "We are not sure that spending all that time on performance management has been yielding a great outcome," Nanterme said in an interview with the *Washington Post*. Wouldn't people perform better if their managers engaged them in frequent conversations about their work? Taking a rather bold step, they ditched the old system in favor of ongoing performance discussions between employees and managers: "We are getting rid of all this comparison with other people," Nanterme declared. The proof of the pudding: In 2018, Accenture reached #60 on *Fortune's* list of the 100 Best Companies to Work For.

In the past you may have been able to show up, punch the clock, go through the motions, and expect an annual raise and Christmas bonus regardless of the results you achieved—those days have ended at most companies. Netflix offers an instructive example. When CEO Reed Hastings wanted to create a performance-driven culture with an intense focus on delivery, he did away with the old subjective "Joe or Jane works *so* hard" system of evaluation and replaced it with one based on the outcomes people achieved. Leaders at Netflix did not care about how hard you worked; they were more interested in the outcomes you generated. You didn't get promoted at Netflix by coming into the office early and leaving late. Hastings wanted the people who made stuff happen, to be the ones who got rewarded.

> *Rewards send signals to employees about what's really valued in the culture.*

Of course, when it comes to culture, one size does not fit all. What works for Facebook or Accenture or Netflix won't necessarily work for you. But whatever system you adopt, make sure that you design it to reward people for getting results. Nordstrom, the high-end US department store, introduced a reward scheme that became known as the "million-dollar club." This approach so generously rewarded entrepreneurial behavior that a top performer could bring home a six-figure salary. The program aligned its incentives with its aspiration that employees think and act like business owners. Sales consultants got to know their customers, kept client lists, and called them when a favorite item of merchandise came into the store. Rewards reinforced the service culture and encouraged a laser-like focus on meeting customer needs.

Employees look to their leaders for signals about what's important and how they should behave. If you want a new culture to stick, you should link rewards to accomplishing the change agenda. That will capture people's attention, sending a powerful signal about what matters most to the organization's leaders. The best reward system communicates that those in charge are not just paying lip service to the need to change the culture; they will reward people who help them get it done.

Notice that I did not say, "*Pay* people who help them get it done." Money talks, but so do other forms of recognition. Sometimes the other forms talk even louder than financial rewards. Psychologists refer to cash payments and promotions as "extrinsic" rewards, meaning that they warm you on the outside. When your boss gives you a 10 percent raise and promotes you to assistant vice president, you can buy more wood for the fire. But that does not necessarily motivate you to earn more wood next quarter. You've got all you need for now. On the other hand, "intrinsic" rewards such as praise and trophies warm you on the inside. When you do something exceptional at work, your boss gives you an "Achievement Award" to recognize your contribution. The glass plaque, with your name etched on the surface, sits on your desk and every time you see it, it reminds you of the awards night and it continues to inspire you to do your best work. Human behavior can be bafflingly complex and you cannot rely on a simple carrot-and-stick approach during change. It is worthwhile spending time exploring how to align "intrinsic" and "extrinsic" rewards with the change objectives. Aligning your processes, policies, and procedures to the desired culture can also accelerate change. And these are the Three Ps.

## ALIGNING THE THREE Ps

Breaking the old patterns in the culture often involves aligning the Three Ps: Processes, Policies, and Procedures. If any of these Three Ps is working against your objectives for the culture, it can slow down or stall your change efforts. The fast-food giant McDonald's found that out the hard way. In late October 2001, the company's CEO, Jack M. Greenberg, stood before a roomful of securities analysts at McDonald's headquarters in Oak Brook, Illinois, fielding a barrage of questions. "Why was McDonald's sitting behind Wendy's and Burger King's customer satisfaction ratings when it had recession-friendly prices and a powerhouse brand?"

Greenberg answered that McDonald's was developing a product to win back customers. Meet Onion McDouble, a new burger loaded with onions, Swiss cheese, and two all-beef patties. The company would introduce the Onion McDouble as part of its "Made For You" strategy, which would invite customers to customize their meals. Freshness would rule. No longer would McDonald's prewrap sandwiches, let them languish in their own juices under heat lamps, or reheat them with microwaves.

"You don't want pickles on your burger? Of course!"

"Hold the ketchup? Certainly!"

"You want extra cheese and onions on that? Absolutely!"

Custom-made and fresh sounded like a smart strategy in the wood-paneled boardroom at Oak Brook, but out in the field it was proving difficult to implement. When Michael Muntzel, who ran four McDonald's franchised outlets in Little Rock, Arkansas, implemented the plan, he ran into trouble. Although he ended up paying $185,000 for a new made-to-order kitchen that headquarters had assured him would cost only $25,000, he figured the investment would pay off in the long run. It didn't. His people couldn't cope with the new labor-intensive process that required triple the time and effort to implement. It was a slow way to make fast food. Frustrated customers, accustomed to superfast service, found themselves standing in long lines waiting, and waiting, and waiting for their meals.

Headquarters had failed to think through the changes that would be required in kitchen processes, procedures, and policies in order to make the new initiative a success. Made For You went against the efficient and reliable culture that McDonald's had spent decades building. And it reduced the bottom line. "It has not produced any new profits for us," Muntzel finally admitted. The failed program ended up costing the company $470 million in kitchen retrofits alone (according to *Forbes*). McDonald's had failed to align the Three Ps (Processes, Policies, and Procedures) with its desired culture.

I first learned the value of the Three Ps when I was living in Sheffield, a city in northern England once famous for steel making, studying for my master's degree in occupational psychology. I had chosen to focus my research on the subject of high-performance teams. Reading books and going to lectures taught me a lot, but I wanted to study a *real* team in action. To that end, I met with Dave Bassett, the manager of the Sheffield United Football Club. I figured football (soccer in the United States) would offer the perfect laboratory for examining how a successful team operates.

I spent the next six months immersed in the daily life of a professional football club, watching the players work out, sitting on the sidelines during matches, and listening to the Monday morning debriefing sessions. I even joined the players for an intensive three-day, military-style boot camp session.

As my research drew to a close, I tried to summarize all that I had learned. No, I did not learn how to score a goal or to head a ball into the back of the net, but I did learn one extremely valuable lesson: Success wasn't about the individual players; it was all about the winning culture in which the players performed. It did not happen by accident. It was the result of carefully designed processes (coaching and drills), policies (putting it all out on the field), and procedures (goal-scoring set plays) conducted by people with a burning desire to win. The coaches did not just manage talent; they aligned the Three Ps in a way that inspired the players to do their best to win championships.

In the business world, the Ritz-Carlton Hotel Company, led by President and COO Herve Humler, offers a prime example of what I'm talking about. Legend has it that a waiter in one of Ritz-Carlton's dining rooms overheard a guest couple's dinnertime conversation in which the woman was lamenting to her husband that they could not use the nearby beach because the access route would not accommodate her wheelchair. The waiter passed the complaint on to the hotel's maintenance team. The following day, management notified the couple that overnight the team had built a wooden bridge from the hotel to the oceanfront. When the couple arrived on the sand that evening, the waiter invited them into a white tent where they enjoyed a romantic candlelit dinner.

The top brass had not told the maintenance team to build the bridge and organize a surprise dinner for the couple. The hotel's people did it because they took to heart a hotel policy that allowed employees to spend up to $2,000 per guest in order to make their stay more enjoyable. Go the extra mile, and guests will return the favor by going out of their way to stay at a Ritz-Carlton Hotel. The team did what they did without even consulting their manager, who did not know about the surprise until the next morning. I've never heard a more heartwarming story about the magic of aligning the Three Ps.

Yes, you need formal, well-thought-out, published policies and procedures. And you need well-oiled processes for getting the job done. Otherwise, chaos can ensue. Work processes that are clear and understood, can help employees to quickly align on how to tackle the task at hand. Policy and procedure documents can help people do their jobs without having to check in with the boss. They help companies manage risk by mandating standards about how employees should conduct themselves. During culture change, they can speed up organizational learning and prevent people from constantly reinventing the wheel. The right documentation can prevent second-guessing, cut through endless discussions, and provide employees with clear guidelines. Another way to provide people with clear guidelines for action, is to redesign the operating model for your business.

*Appropriate policies and procedures can speed up organizational learning during culture change.*

## REMODELING THE BUSINESS

Breaking out of old habits invariably requires some shifts to your business model. Shifts come in all sizes, from small process improvements to a complete reshaping of the way a company does business. But you must take care that you don't simply rearrange the deck chairs on your ship while it continues to sink in a sea of red ink. Organizational restructures can move people around, without producing any real transformation. After all the navel gazing, people may go back to their old ways of doing things and the dysfunctional patterns continue. Nike's 2008 restructure, designed to create a more agile and growth-oriented culture, offers an excellent case in point. Nike had originally structured itself around product lines, with various departments selling equipment, apparel, and footwear. When Nike's leaders realized that consumers wanted to buy complete outfits appropriate for their favorite sport, they decided to restructure along sports categories.

Nike's leaders sat back and waited for the results of this thoughtful remodel. Surely, customers would love it. But they didn't. Despite some early gains, they watched sales continue to sag. They had restructured the business, but they had not fixed the real problem: shoe styles their customers found outdated and boring. Archrival Adidas was pulling in more and more customers with its aggressive, almost-weekly introduction of cool retro models, eye-popping futuristic designs, and sneakers with killer looks. Struggling to compete, Nike went back to the drawing board and came up with yet another massive restructure in 2017, this time cutting styles and its workforce. They also copied a two-year-old Adidas strategy by announcing a focus on "deeply serving customers" in twelve cities. They forgot one thing. Adidas had reframed the role of employees as "trendsetters." Nike's layoffs, on the other hand, had thrown the fear of job loss into the minds of its employees. Nike hoped to reverse the tide in 2018 with a new cutting-edge 68,000-square-foot flagship store in New York City that offered customized sneakers and digital shopping.

*Restructures give leaders the opportunity to fast-track change by reframing the role of different parts of the organization.*

Leaders who bring about real and lasting change by remodeling their business do not just imitate their rivals or jump on the latest organizational theory. They bring imagination and a passion for inspiring their people and delighting their customers to the undertaking.

Satya Nadella did just that when he became CEO at Microsoft in 2014, inheriting an organization that had stopped producing trailblazing products. Realizing that he needed to steer the company into a post-PC, cloud-centric era, Nadella launched a major restructure aimed at moving Microsoft away from selling packaged software to offering subscription-based cloud services. This move not only responded to the shifting marketplace, it attacked the old Microsoft culture that suffered from too much unproductive, internal competition.

The restructure connected people to a new purpose-driven cause by grouping all products into wider organizational units, each with a specific role, such as "building the intelligent cloud platform" or "creating more personal computing." As the CEO explained in an email to employees: "Perhaps the most important driver of success is culture. Over the past year we've challenged ourselves to think about our core mission, our soul—what would be lost if we disappeared. . . . We also asked ourselves what culture we want to foster that will enable us to achieve these goals."

The restructure took a lot of courage. It meant massive layoffs and the dissolution and write-off of the Nokia acquisition to the tune of $7.6 billion, according to *Forbes*. But soon a more collaborative, friendly, and less fearful culture emerged. A company that had once disdained and driven away potential partners began forging partnerships with such outfits as Red Hat, Salesforce, and even Amazon. It also began introducing new technologies: an enhanced Xbox experience, the GigJam collaboration tool, and new products, such as Office for iPad and Office 365, that captured a lot of new customers. By October 2018, more than two-thirds of Microsoft's revenue was pouring in from reoccurring subscription services. According to the *New York Times*, in 2019, Microsoft hit a $1 trillion market valuation (joining Apple and Amazon). Microsoft's share price had begun to soar, and according to CNBC, it tripled from 2014 to mid-2018, as investors jumped aboard the remodeled company.

Nadella's business remodel had broken the old ways in the Microsoft culture and made all that happen. It led to happy customers and investors, and it also created a collaborative workplace where employees worked hard to achieve the company's mission.

## TAILORING WORKSPACES
## TO SUIT THE CULTURE

You can hire architects, builders, and interior designers to create physical workspaces, but you won't end up with an environment that fully engages people in the change, if you do not match the space to the culture you are creating. The setting in which the work takes place must go beyond four walls and a bank of windows, it must inspire people to act in ways that match the espoused values in your culture. A stroll around Google's offices reveals unusual and offbeat office designs that encourage employee creativity. People glide around campus on scooters, bring their dogs to work, or take a break at the Google bowling alley. You want to exercise while you code? Here, put a treadmill beside your stand-up desk. Your meeting room is not a walled-in cubicle but a ski cabin in Zurich, a sidewalk café in Istanbul, or a vintage New York subway car. These and other innovative attempts to create ideal workspaces have taken Google a long way toward realizing its mission to become the "happiest, most productive workplace in the world."

Another example was my client "Claudia Harrison," the cofounder of "HarrisonRockAccountants," a medium-sized accounting firm based in London, with a reputation for good service at reasonable rates. Claudia sought my advice about how to create a more collaborative culture in her workplace. When we caught up for coffee she explained how business was booming but that the office space was no longer meeting her needs: "I'm fed up with the rabbit warren layout of our premises. Employees are hidden away in offices and rarely talk or exchange ideas."

I nodded: "Sounds like you've outgrown the place. You could relocate and use the move to trigger a shift to a more collaborative culture."

Claudia went searching and found the perfect premises with plenty of space and views over the river Thames. She worked with an interior designer on her vision to create a more collaborative culture and six months later she invited me on a tour of the premises. The new office was light years away from the old building where people were crammed into dark offices and surrounded by filing cabinets. Claudia had created a large open plan space, filled with natural light.

I asked her, "Where's your corner office?"

Claudia responded: "I hated that corner office. It was just incredibly isolating."

If Claudia needed to hold a private conversation, she took the discussion to a closed room called a "quiet room." She had studied open office plans before she decided to adopt one for her company: "As I looked at these places, there was just this energy, buzz and sense of excitement of collaborative human endeavor that really was kind of exhilarating." Furthermore, she thought the company would benefit from having its cofounder out in the mix with the rest of the employees.

As we made our way around the floor Claudia explained, "There are dedicated areas for printers and photocopiers on each level, so people get up from their desks to use shared utility spaces." Glass walls allowed people to see each other as they moved around the floors. A wide stairwell, between floors, encouraged people to walk rather than use the lifts. Employees at HarrisonRock now spent their lunchtimes sitting and chatting in the bright, spacious kitchen area. The new workspace was a far cry from the old building and encouraged a shift to a more collaborative culture. The end result: clients reported higher levels of satisfaction with the ideas and advice they were receiving from employees—who were sharing and learning more from each other.

*Smart leaders reflect the culture in the look*
*and feel of the workplace.*

Astute leaders know that the setting in which the work takes place can have a major impact on how people think, feel, and interact in the workplace.

## · POINTS TO REMEMBER ·

- You can accelerate culture change by aligning your systems to the desired culture.
- Technological advancements should always include the human factor.
- People need both extrinsic and intrinsic rewards.
- Processes, policies, and procedures must align with your aspiration for the culture.
- A new business model can help to accelerate change, by reframing the roles of different parts of the business.
- Physical spaces affect the way people think and act.

# 9

## GATHER
## CHANGE MOMENTUM

### Enabling the
### Change to Spread Rapidly

You will recall from earlier chapters that the Australian bank, ANZ had at one time completely lost the trust of its customers and the communities it served. While the new CEO, John McFarlane, took many steps to regain that trust, none made a stronger and more lasting impression on everyone than his announcement that ANZ would buy fifty-six local branches a competitor had closed because those operations were not contributing enough to corporate profits. It turned out that ANZ could not consummate the promised purchase, but McFarlane issued the order that the bank would not close any more rural branches. That was welcome news. The public viewed all branch closings as just another example of a banking industry that did not care about the needs of customers. The banks were adapting to the most significant technological shift in their history, but not all their customers were liking the move away from traditional face-face-face banking to electronic banking. According to an Australian Parliamentary report, the number of banks in Australia fell by one-third in a eight-year period, between 1993 and 2000.

People in remote areas were hardest hit and many struggled with the l oss of full banking services. McFarlane showed he cared, by declaring a stop to further bank closures and setting up mobile banking services in remote regions.

These decisions signaled to employees that this was a change they could believe in and a leader they could trust to fulfil his promise of "a bank with a human face." The change started to gather momentum, as the skeptics came on board. Now there were more people who believed in the change, than were against it. The bestselling author, Malcolm Gladwell, refers to this shift as the "tipping point," when little things can make a big difference.

In scientific terms, a tipping point represents a threshold at which an infectious disease spirals out of control and runs rapidly though a community. In culture terms, it is that point at which the new culture begins to take on a life of its own, spreading like wildfire as it captures an increasing number of employees, customers, and community leaders until it becomes "how things work around here." The change has gone viral. Nothing can stop it now.

In the third step of change, your aim is to break out of the patterns that no longer serve you and reach that crucial tipping point. To reach this point where the game changes completely, leaders must first deal with the change blockers.

## DEALING WITH THE BLOCKERS

"Maria Jones" was an executive in the hospitality industry who was in charge of an ambitious plan to roll out a series of new restaurants across the country. Marie wanted to create a culture of high-performance and employee well-being in her team, and asked to meet with me to pick my brain on how she should proceed. We met in her local café, overlooking the ocean on Australia's Gold Coast and Maria explained, "I need my team to have the stamina for a big year ahead—high performance and well-being are critical to our success and our values." We got chatting about Maria's own well-being goals and she admitted, "I want to learn sea kayaking, but I haven't had one lesson yet."

"What's stopping you?' I asked.

"I'm not quite sure," Maria responded. "I start every week with good intentions, but work's been busy."

I asked, "Do you have any fears or concerns about kayaking?"

Maria quipped, "No concerns, just not enough time!"

Despite her initial response, Maria agreed to reflect on any concerns she might have about kayaking before our next session. We met a week later and before I could sit down Maria began: "You know you asked about my fears. Well I'd completely forgotten this, but I've been terrified of sharks ever since I was a child!"

We spent the rest of the session exploring how Maria's unconscious fear of sharks was preventing her from reaching her well-being goal. In the end, she decided to join a beginner's club that kayaked in local rivers (where sharks rarely ventured). Six months later she was hitting the key milestones on her new restaurant roll-out plan *and* she was sticking to her kayaking regime.

Not all assumptions are as dramatic as Maria's fear of sharks. However, they can still prevent individuals and organizations from changing. These assumptions, held at the collective level, can show up as resistance to change: "That's not how things work around here." Tackling these assumptions is vital in order to accelerate change during the third step (*Break* the patterns) on The Culture Disruptor.

The Harvard professor Dr. Robert Kegan spent his career researching why people so often fail to change. Why on earth, he wondered, would six out of seven heart patients stick with their old bad habits, such as an unhealthy diet, too little exercise, and smoking, when their doctors have told them their old habits would kill them? It turned out that, despite the threat of death, a heart patient may know he should do the right thing but falls back on bad habits because that's not how he has always lived his life. "I can't do it that way because that's not how I do things around here."

That's why it's so hard to change human behavior. You can't just tell people to do the right thing; you must tackle their underlying assumptions ("I might get bitten by a shark" or "I can't get going in the morning without a cigarette"). These assumptions can be hard to detect, like the body of an iceberg. Above the surface of the water, an iceberg can look pretty small, but underneath you'll find a mass of ice that can sink the *Titanic*. On April 10, 1912, the largest ship ever built (at that time) embarked on its maiden voyage from Southampton to

New York, its passengers delighted with the luxurious accommodations and looking forward to a smooth and problem-free cruise. Those hopes were shattered when, four days into the voyage, the ship collided with an iceberg's jagged underwater spur that tore a three-hundred-foot gash in the side of the *Titanic*. How could a supposedly unsinkable ship go down in the icy waters of the North Atlantic, taking the lives of more than fifteen hundred people? You could ask the same question when supposedly "too big to fail" companies like Goldman Sachs get into trouble. Look closely enough, and you'll see that culture (and the deeply embedded assumptions that sustain the culture) was a key causal factor. What assumptions threaten your organization?

The reaction of taxi drivers to the emergence of Uber offers a classic example of how assumptions can prevent people from changing. On June 11, 2014, five thousand taxi drivers paralyzed London's city center in a fight to save them from the Uber threat. The protesters objected to the upstart ride-hailing competitor whose drivers, they argued, lacked "The Knowledge" (a grueling two- to four-year test of London streets that all cabbies needed to pass). The protest failed. Fed-up passengers, it turned out, cared more about the convenience Uber offered than they did about driver knowledge. The old-fashioned cabbies, unable to change their long-standing assumptions about their business, faced certain doom.

Consider just one of those deadly assumptions. When a *Financial Times* reporter interviewed a London taxi driver about the threat, the cabbie responded: "We have been here long before Uber and we will be here long after." The assumption that "we will be here forever" contributed to a complacency that outraged passengers who were sick and tired of long waits, rude drivers, dirty vehicles, and longer-than-necessary routes to their destinations. When Uber founder Travis Kalanick faced these conditions when trying to hail a taxi in Paris in 2008 he had a eureka moment—tap a button, get a ride. It turned out to be one of the most game-changing ideas in modern business history. Creating his business on a new set of assumptions, Kalanick went on to build a company that *Fast Company* dubbed one of the "most innovative companies" in 2017 and, as of 2018, was worth an impressive $72 billion.

The assumptions, held at a collective level in the culture, can serve to protect the organization against the potential dangers that change can bring. However, these assumptions can also stop you from adapting and growing. Take the Japanese company Toshiba as an example. Toshiba traced its roots to 1875, when Tanaka Hisashige, the eldest son of a Japanese tortoiseshell craftsman, founded what would become a global business giant. Tanaka, known as the "Thomas Edison of Japan," had invented everything from looms, clockwork dolls, and oil lamps to Japan's first steam locomotive. The founder's innovative spirit infused the company's DNA. The Toshiba Corporation continued to grow through the first half of the twentieth century, developing videotape recorders, television sets, air conditioners, and mail-processing equipment. In the late 1980s, Toshiba computers filled the shelves of retailers around the world and quickly captured 17.7 percent of all computer sales in the United States.

However, the reverence employees held for the firm's legendary founder evolved into a dangerous change-immune assumption: "Do whatever it takes to please the boss." This assumption engendered a generation of "yes men" who did not actually follow their founder's example. Moving in lockstep, they failed to keep innovating in a marketplace filled with agile and disruptive rivals. A culture where managers feared delivering bad news to company leaders led to a 2015 scandal when company officials overstated profits for the failing personal computing business by $1.2 billion, (according to *Reuters*). Toshiba's woes didn't stop there and in 2016, the company made a shock announcement of an unexpected loss of $6.3 billion at its US nuclear business (according to the BBC). These scandals revealed how an assumption—"we must hide bad news from the boss"—could end up ruining a business. Toshiba is still operating but is no longer running its personal computing business, and its US nuclear business (Westinghouse) has filed for bankruptcy. History often reveals uncomfortable truths. If you want to identify and change the deeply embedded assumptions that could threaten your organization's change efforts, you should take a long, hard look at the reasons behind those assumptions.

• • •

## UNDERSTANDING THE REASONS
## FOR YOUR CULTURE'S ASSUMPTIONS

Before you can overturn the assumptions that are blocking your culture change efforts, you must first discover the reasons these assumptions developed in the first place. Clinton Cards, once the United Kingdom's largest greeting card company, offers a good case in point. According to the *Daily Mail*, in the late 1960s, Don Lewis, the son of an East London chimney sweep, took his £500 savings and opened his first card shop on Epping High Street, London. Lewis initially hoped to earn just enough money to buy a Rolls-Royce, but he went on to become the multimillionaire kingpin of a thousand-plus-store network, with a presence in high streets across Britian. With £3 cards costing as little as 30p to manufacture, Lewis had developed a formidable profit machine.

So why was Clinton Cards teetering on the brink of collapse in 2012, with the fate of its eight thousand employees hanging in the balance? You can guess the reason: a flawed assumption. The leadership at Clinton Cards assumed that the British public would always buy physical greeting cards, while, in fact, technology was shifting in favor of online retailers, such as Jacquie Lawson. Why drive to a shop for Uncle Benny's birthday card, when you could send him a beautiful electronic card with a few clicks of your mouse? The clincher? In 2018, a full year's subscription to Jacquie Lawson allowed a subscriber to send an unlimited number of cards for a mere £9 per year.

Why do company leaders so often fail to see and react to the threats and opportunities in the marketplace? Well, it usually involves some basic beliefs or unchallenged assumptions that have been guiding decision making. Take the Concorde aircraft, for example. After an auspicious debut, the super-large, superfast plane eventually went the way of the dodo bird. The first British Airway's Concorde entered service in 1976 with a flight to the tiny Persian Gulf state of Bahrain, reaching a cruising altitude of 19,812 meters (twice the height of other airliners) and a speed of 1,345 mph (more than twice the speed of sound). British newspaper headlines heralded the achievement: "Triumphant Debut by Concorde: This without doubt must be the greatest leap forward in air travel the world has ever known."

Yes, the Concorde could fly a hundred passengers from London to New York in just three and a half hours, but folks on the ground below the plane were finding their ears battered by sonic booms. That did not deter British Airways and British government officials from pleading with the Americans to let their plane visit New York. After all, the Brits needed to recoup their huge investment in the aircraft. Development of the Concorde had cost fifteen times the original estimate, and maintenance costs had soared through the stratosphere, making it necessary to charge passengers more than thirty times the cost of a nonsupersonic flight.

Although these problems became apparent early on, they could not deter British government officials from pursuing the Concorde dream for almost thirty years. Call it "death by assumption." In this case, the cause was the belief that a groundbreaking aircraft would prove Britain's prowess in the global aviation industry. The plane won a lot of admiration, snagging first prize in the 2006 Great British Design Quest competition and winning the applause of many aircraft aficionados. But, weighed down by far too much financial, environmental, and political baggage, the emblem of British air dominance was eventually retired. The assumptions in your organization, have developed for a very vaild reason. Find out why they have emerged and you will have the key to successfully overturning them.

Gathering change momemtum often means overturning collective and deeply held assumptions. Ben Harkness, the CEO at BuildItPro, was struggling to reach a point where the change, to a more accountable and innovative culture, was spreading rapidly. To accelerate the change, he and I first hosted a series of workshops with BuildItPro managers aimed specifically at unearthing the old assumptions that were blocking change.

Ever since its founding by an Italian family in the 1950s, BuildItPro had attracted clients with its can-do approach to business. That attitude sprang in part from the founders' bringing whole families from their native town in southern Italy to support the company's rapidly expanding business. These immigrants, grateful for their new homes in America, eagerly joined BuildItPro's extended family. A basic assumption developed: "The company will take care of us, no matter what."

The company's culture centered on reciprocal loyalty and a fierce esprit de corps. In the early days of rapid expansion, close bonds developed between employees at BuildItPro. These strong relationships helped them to survive in a new country and to get the job done on challenging construction projects in far-flung locations. Another assumption developed, in this family culture, that *"you need to fit in and be liked around here."* This assumption ultimately led employees to value their relationships at work, more than their performance on the job. The business suffered as a result. People were taking shortcuts, letting standards slip, and ignoring the industry's rules and regulations. Rather than replacing underperformers, management simply moved them from one project to another, hoping those who performed poorly would do minimal damage. Managers did not want to fire people they viewed like their brothers and sisters. Somehow, we needed to reframe roles from "family members" to "work colleagues."

During the workshops, we encouraged managers to question the old assumptions and to determine whether they still made sense. It began to dawn on the managers that you do not do employees a favor by ignoring their poor performance. On the other hand, you do them a real favor when you coach them to better performance or release them to look elsewhere for more satisfying work. That idea set the stage for a new assumption: "In this company, everyone must carry their weight." The workshops reframed the role of managers and helped overturn the old assumptions that were blocking change. The managers stepped up to break the old pattern and started to hold people to account for performance outcomes. BuildItPro began to become a more performance-focused culture and the gathering change momentum showed up in improved financial performance—a year later the company reported a profit for the first time in several years.

Gathering momentum on the change journey can feel like an uphill battle. For the change to spread rapidly, you will need to get past middle management.

## GETTING PAST MIDDLE MANAGEMENT

While organizational leaders are warming to the idea of change, the middle management layer can remain unconvinced about the merits of transforming. Unless you get middle managers on board, you will see very little meaningful change at the front lines of your business.

John Flannery, an ex-CEO at General Electric, learned this lesson the hard way. In 2017, GE, hobbled by debt (caused by years of bad decisions) and an underperforming power division (in total disarray), desperately needed culture change. To engineer the required turnaround, the board appointed Flannery to lead the effort. But something went terribly wrong, and GE shocked the business community a little over a year later, when it announced that it would replace Flannery with a new CEO.

Where had Flannery gone wrong? It turned out that he had underestimated how strongly middle managers at GE would resist changing "how things work around here." When Flannery's turnaround message did not get through to the people who managed GE's 300,000 employees, the company lost a breathtaking $124 billion in value during Flannery's first year in office. The board took drastic action. As Todd Lowenstein, a fund manager at Highmark Capital Management (which owned a lot of GE shares), said, "Investors and the board obviously lost patience with the glacial turnaround plan, mis-execution, and poor communications."

In 2018, the board replaced Flannery with Larry Culp, the first outsider to hold the top job in GE's 126-year history. Culp brought strong culture credentials to the role. In his previous job at Danaher, another globally powerful conglomerate, he had built what some observers called a "cult-like culture." That may sound a little scary, but Culp's approach did get results. Rather than communicating with his middle managers in long, boring meetings, he visited them where they worked. A *Wall Street Journal* article described how he would don his steel-capped safety shoes and walk the factory floor, talking to managers and their people about the issues they faced. Culp posted daily notes on the company's intranet, praising staff for the improvements he witnessed on his rounds. The GE board were anticipating a similar approach would help restore GE's reputation to its glory days, when its culture was considered one of the most vibrant and productive in the world.

Getting your change messages through to front line staff often comes down to communication. Consider how a communications strategy worked for HubSpot, the Massachusetts-based software company founded in 2005 by Dharmesh Shah and Brian Halligan while they were still enrolled as graduate students at MIT. The two entrepreneurs had a vision to create an all-in-one software tool that would allow customers to manage every aspect of their marketing campaigns. They realized that vision. By 2018, the company was employing two thousand employees serving fifty-two thousand customers.

As the company grew, the founders struggled to maintain the sort of open and transparent culture they believed they needed to run a successful global business. Cofounder Dharmesh Shah, who describes himself as an introvert, was concerned that (as HubSpot grew) staff might not be receiving enough direct communication from him. So he launched an initiative called "Ask Dharmesh Anything," where people could pose any question to the cofounder and he would publish the answers online:

> **Ethan:** Hi Dharmesh! I am in my second round interview for an IMC position (at HubSpot). How can I demonstrate I am a top performer?
>
> **Darmesh:** Here are some tips:
>   1. Show how you will care maniacally about customer happiness.
>   2. Demonstrate a desire to be constantly learning. Our world changes fast.
>   3. Be human. Be self-aware. Be nice.
>
> Best wishes with the interview.

To build HubSpot's aspirational, open and transparent culture, Shah stepped out of his role as the "I feel uncomfortable talking to people" nerd and into the role of "communicator." That one small reframe paid dividends. In 2017, HubSpot reported revenues of $356.7 million, up 40 percent over the prior year. As for the people who worked there, they felt so engaged that the company took the #1 spot on Comparably's 2018 "Best Company for Employee Happiness" list.

I recall working with "Theresa Martinez," an executive in the retail organization "DressSmart." Theresa wanted to create a more customer-oriented culture across her stores, but her best efforts had done nothing to accomplish that goal. A bit stuck, she called me from the airport as she waited to board her flight home after a whirlwind tour of her retail outlets. "I need your advice," she exclaimed, "my frontline staff have no idea about the need for change that I've been talking about for months!"

Hmm. I'd heard that complaint before from many managers. We arranged to meet the following day in Theresa's office. As I took notes, she explained the downward trend in customer satisfaction ratings despite all the time she spent communicating the need for DressSmart to become a much more customer-friendly organization. "I've visited the stores twice already this year but all I see is the same old, same old behavior. If I can't turn this around, my boss, Svetlana, will be looking for my replacement."

I suggested, "Maybe you're doing too much communicating."

Theresa's eyes widened. "What? That's not possible!"

"Sometimes it is! Let me explain. You seem to have stepped into the role of the middle managers and are doing the communicating *for* them. You're letting them off the hook. Perhaps it's time for a role reframe."

I explained to Theresa that it was important to put the middle managers into their communication role, to carry the change messages to employees in the stores. The store managers needed to stop taking up the role of "observers" and start stepping into the role of "communicators."

*Successful change depends on middle managers communicating the message to the front line.*

Theresa got it. "OK! I'm going to stop compensating for the lack of communication by my store managers and put the onus on them to deliver the change messages." She did just that. Then she monitored progress. Sure enough, within six months she could see with her own eyes a marked improvement in customer service in the stores. Her managers were happy, the shop clerks were happy, and Theresa was happy. All it took was to invite the store managers to take up their role to communicate the culture change imperatives to employees.

It's a transformational story. And stories are powerful ways to engage and mobilize people during culture change. As the Native American proverb says, "Tell me the facts and I'll learn. Tell me the truth and I'll believe. But tell me a story and it will live in my heart forever."

●　　●　　●

## CHANGING THE STORY

Since ancient times humans have gathered around fires to share stories. These stories represent our cultural heritage. The ancient stories of Greek heroines Antigone and Athena, *The Iliad* and other tales originally recited by Homer—these stories codified the values of courage, hospitality, and respect so prized by the ancient Greeks. In today's business world, stories teach similarly valuable lessons.

Patience: James Dyson created the bagless vacuum cleaner after a staggering 5,127 prototypes.

Perseverance: A penniless sixty-five-year-old Colonel Sanders received more than a thousand rejections for his chicken recipe before a restaurant owner finally gave him a chance.

Imagination: The 3M scientist Art Fry, codeveloper of Post-it Notes, came up with the perfect use for a new adhesive when he needed a temporary bookmark in his hymnal at church.

We share stories in the workplace every day, often with little or no thought about how they relate to our organization's culture. Shift supervisor Kelly tells her colleagues in the lunchroom about her latest skirmish over the pay deal with upper management. Entrepreneur Isabella describes her vision for a new digital assistant for children to a rapt audience of potential investors. Jeremiah, an insurance company employee, warns a customer that a flood could severely damage her property with a tale of a recent storm. Leaders intent on culture transformation can harness the organization's stories in the service of the change.

The CEO of Walmart, Doug McMillon, tapped the power of storytelling when he opened the company's 2015 annual shareholder meeting with the declaration, "At Walmart, we love stories. There is just something about them. We enjoy telling them. We love hearing them. We repeat stories and pass them down. We also write them. Together we're writing our company's story."

McMillon commissioned famous moviemakers, including Seth Rogen and Evan Goldberg, to create a new Walmart ad campaign based on storytelling. The ads revolved around popular items purchased by Walmart shoppers from bananas and paper towels to batteries and toys. McMillon gave the directors one simple direction: tell stories that showcase our culture.

Filmmakers showed the first of the sixty-second ads, "Banana Town," during the eighty-ninth annual Academy Awards. The imaginative, uplifting singing and dancing romp delivered the message that "every receipt tells a story." McMillon's storytelling communications strategy rang a bell with customers and employees alike. In 2018, Walmart employees performed far beyond market expectations, delivering revenues of $500 billion in 2018, with US online sales up an impressive 33 percent (according to CNBC).

You may not be able to afford a Hollywood scriptwriter or director to tell your organization's stories, but you can write and collect and tell the stories that break the old habits and bring your new culture to life. Pick and choose the ones that work best; discard those that run counter to the values of the culture. When Tim Cook took over from Steve Jobs as Apple's CEO, he shared a story about growing up in Alabama. Cycling home one night, he saw a cross burning outside a black family's home, with a circle of hooded Klansmen surrounding it. When Cook shouted, "No!" one of the Klansmen lifted his hood to reveal a familiar face, a deacon at Cook's church. "Growing up in Alabama in the 1960s I saw the devastating effect of discrimination and it would change my life forever. For me, the cross-burning was a symbol of ignorance, of hatred, and a fear of anyone different than the majority." Cook did not share this incident in an effort to present himself as a believer in diversity and an opponent of racism. He told the story to underscore Apple's cultural commitment to "respect for human dignity."

Early experiences often shape a leader's signature culture story. Yvon Chouinard, the cofounder of the outdoor outfitter Patagonia, tells how he went from hippie to reluctant businessman. An avid rock climber in the 1960s, he rebelled against authority and took pride in calling himself a "dirtbag" who spent two hundred nights a year sleeping outdoors. "I never wanted to be a conventional businessman. I liked climbing rocks, not corporate ladders." Chouinard went on to build a corporate empire with a culture imbued with his passion for sustainable living and environmental protection.

On Black Friday 2011, the day Americans begin the frantic Christmas shopping season (so named because it helps so many companies produce black ink on their balance sheets), Chouinard ran a full-page ad in the *New York Times* proclaiming, "Don't buy this jacket." People should, the ad suggested, buy only what they absolutely needed. When Patagonia sold out its entire inventory of the jackets, Chouinard made a pact with customers that if they had purchased one, the company would repair it forever. "Repair it. Reuse it. Recycle it."

Rose Marcario became CEO of Patagonia in 2014 (having joined as CFO in 2008) and she has remained true to the founder's story and the vision to create a truly sustainable culture. For the 2016 Black Friday campaign, Marcario promised to donate to charity every dollar in revenues the company reaped that day, eventually more than $10 million. She continued to donate 1 percent of Patagonia's profits to grassroots environmental groups and by 2018, the company had gifted more than $75 million to environmental causes. Supportive customers spread the word to family and friends, resulting in revenues in excess of $1 billion in 2017—more than triple the profits since Marcario was hired (according to *Fast Company*).

> *Tell me a story and it will live in my heart forever.*
> *—Native American proverb*

Crafting and telling relevant culture stories provides one of the best tools leaders can use to foster change. They can galvanize people at the beginning of the change effort, accelerate change to help reach the tipping point, and propel people in a new direction, if and when the organization needs to transform its culture again. The best ones employ powerful symbols to capture the imagination.

## EMPLOYING POWERFUL SYMBOLS TO REINFORCE THE CHANGE

Symbolism is the art of using an object or a word to represent an abstract idea. Cultural traits, such as "agile" or "innovative" or "accountable," are abstract ideas. As the learning theorist Piaget pointed out, people more easily grasp abstract ideas when they can picture an example in their mind's eye. For instance, if I want you to think about a concept such as "beauty" or "love," I will plant an image in your mind: "one perfect red rose" or "Jane holding her newborn daughter."

Organizational symbols can help you gain change momentum because they help people remember the new cultural traits and break out of the old ways. Symbols take many forms, from the famous white-shirt-and-black-tie dress code IBM employed in its early days, to the US Marine Corps' memorable slogan "Semper Fi." Spacesaver, a leader in commercial storage, understood the power of symbols to help it create its customer-focused culture. Theodore W. Batterman founded the company in 1972 with seven employees in a 10,000-square-foot barn in Fort Atkinson, Wisconsin. Wanting to help companies solve problems associated with space and energy conservation, he spearheaded the development of high-density storage and shelving in the United States.

At the Field Museum, Chicago, one of Spacesaver's early clients, two hundred scientists dealt daily with some 2.2 million objects and specimens. When the museum ran out of space, Spacesaver came to the rescue, designing a new $65 million, underground 180,000-square-foot storage facility. This incredibly complex project, involving 274 moveable carriages and more than 2,700 sections of shelving, beautifully solved the problem.

The leaders at Spacesaver used this accomplishment to drive home to their people the company's central cultural trait: the idea that customers' needs should guide them to provide the most effective and the most creative solutions to its customers' problems. When employees came to work one day, they saw massive photos of dinosaur skulls and bones stored on the storage system Spacesaver had designed and installed at the Field Museum. Everyone could see customer service in action. Fueled by its customer-centric culture, Spacesaver, now part of the K1 Group, helped the Group to notch up sales of $700 million in 2018.

You can make yourself hoarse talking about creating great customer experiences, but you can save a lot of breath if you use well-crafted symbols to replace all of that long-winded verbiage employees will forget the minute you stop talking. Jeff Bezos knew how to do that. He once said, "Obsessing over customer experience is the only long-term defensible competitive advantage." In order to make that concept tangible and memorable, Bezos directed anyone convening a meeting at the company to place an empty chair in the room. That vacant chair represented the customer, "the most important person in the room."

There's a lot of "noise" in any workplace. The explosion of data, the clamoring of social media, and the bewildering pace of technological change can make it hard to see what's really important. The right symbols can cut through all that noise and signal a shift to a new culture. Take for instance, the leaders at FedEx, who wanted to create a safety culture among its 400,000 employees. These staff members delivered more than 10 million packages to customers in more than 220 countries every day. The leaders came up with a powerful symbol to reinforce the safety culture: a bright orange seat belt installed in each one of its 100,000 trucks. The executives could have given detailed presentations about road safety to their drivers, but they found a much better way to get their people thinking about safe driving. FedEx estimated that wearing a seatbelt reduced the risk of its drivers suffering a fatal injury by 45 percent. The orange belt worked because people could see the safety focus at FedEx every time they buckled up.

Try making a list of the cultural traits you want your people to embrace. For each of them, create in your mind's eye a picture of that abstract quality. You want positivity? Install a bell that's rung every time your team has a major win. You want teamwork? Create a high-profile Collaboration award. You want customer focus? Implement a new rule: We talk to three customers every week.

Dealing with the hidden assumptions, getting through the middle management layer, and deploying symbols and stories can help you accelerate the change and move from the third to the fourth step of culture change (*Consolidate* the gains).

## · POINTS TO REMEMBER ·

- Any culture change initiative must deal with the hidden assumptions.
- The assumptions in your culture have developed for a reason.
- Change can get stuck in the middle management layer of the organization.
- Transformation depends on middle managers stepping into their communication role, to deliver the change messages to the front line.
- Compelling stories build change momentum.
- Powerful symbols can help break out of the old ways and bring the new culture to life.

# 10

## CONSOLIDATE GAINS

### Embedding the Emerging Culture

Jørn Lyseggen, the founder of the business intelligence and media monitoring company Meltwater, was born in South Korea and later adopted by a Norwegian family and raised on a small farm near the Swedish border. Meltwater's story began in Oslo in 2001 (just after the dotcom bubble burst) when Lyseggen rented an office in Oslo's shipyard and invested $15,000 to develop software that would enable businesses to gather vital information ranging from what people were saying about them on social media to the activities of their competitors. Within a few years, Meltwater became one of the largest media intelligence companies in the world, with more than thirty thousand clients in 108 countries. The list included such diverse clients as the Harvard Business School, Coca-Cola, Air France, the Muhammad Ali Center, and Jersey Mike's.

Meltwater's success stemmed in large part from a vibrant culture expressed by a simple three-letter acronym, MER, the Norwegian word for "more." MER (according to the company's website) reminds employees to keep the company's core values in mind:

- *Moro* or "fun." Lyseggen believes that successful people enjoy their work.
- *Enere* or "number one." No employee should ever settle for average results but should constantly strive to exceed his or her own expectations.
- *Respekt* or "respect." People work harder and get better results when they follow the Golden Rule, treating colleagues the way they themselves would like to be treated.

With this set of values in place, Lyseggen and his team built a version of Google Alerts (before Google Alerts), software that could scan billions of online conversations, extract relevant insights from the World Wide Web, and provide clients with information that could help them enhance their brands. According to *Forbes*, by 2017, the company was producing annual revenues approaching $300 million, with a 15 percent profit margin. MER helped Meltwater consolidate its gains, year after year after year.

> *Consolidate (verb): Make (something) physically stronger or more solid; strengthen a position of power or success, so that it is more likely to continue.*

Any leader intent on building a similarly successful culture must also embed the culture, the fourth step on The Culture Disruptor, *Consolidate* the gains (depicted by an upward spiral in Figure 10.1).

When someone asks me how long it takes to change workplace culture, I usually say, "It depends." It will vary according to a myriad factors: the strength of the existing culture, the size of the organization, the assumptions in the culture, and how deeply embedded the patterns are, just to name a few. In smaller organizations (or teams), you can achieve a lot in as little as a year, while in large organizations it might take three or more years to make the transformation. In either case, you must maintain unswerving dedication to the change effort.

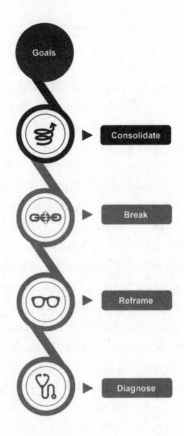

Figure 10.1. The Fourth Step on The Culture Disruptor: Consolidate Your Gains

## MAINTAINING AN UNSWERVING DEDICATION TO THE CHANGE EFFORT

One of the biggest issues during culture transformation is that leaders can lose momentum on the journey. After an initial burst of energy, you may lose some of your passion for the change and fall back into the old ways of doing things. If that happens, you might take a cue from successful professional sports teams. Perennial winners, such as the New England Patriots during the years they dominated the National Football League, work hard to consolidate their gains every year. Coach Bill Belichick and quarterback Tom Brady understood the need for a rallying cry that would help teammates dedicate themselves to doing whatever it took to win championships: "Do your job."

In the world of professional cycling, no one did their jobs better than the members of Team Sky. For several years, they dominated the Tour de France, one of the world's longest and most grueling cycling competitions. Imagine riding a bike 2,100 miles in twenty-three days. You need more than physical strength to win the race. You need a team of individuals all dedicated to stepping into their roles: the *domestique* (a companion rider who sacrifices himself for the good of the team by riding in front of the main rider to reduce wind drag); the *seigneurs* (massage therapists who provide physical therapy as well as maintain supplies of food and drink for the riders); the *mecaniques* (skilled technicians who keep the bikes in perfect condition and can change a damaged tire in seconds); the *chef* (a specialist in high-performance nutrition); and a team of other key support staff. To win a tough race like the Tour de France (according to the cycling website *road.cc*), you must concentrate on three things: details, details, and more details. Team Sky's attention-to-detail culture helped it win its sixth Tour de France championship in 2018.

In the business world, accommodation-facilitator Airbnb's cofounder Brian Chesky knew the value of keeping your foot on the accelerator. On Monday, October 21, 2013 (according to his Twitter post), Chesky sent a memo to his people with a startling subject line: "Don't f*ck up the culture." This stemmed from something investor Peter Thiel had said about his reason for putting $150 million into the company: Airbnb's culture. In his note to employees, Chesky reminded everyone: "The thing that will endure for 100 years, the way it has for most 100-year companies, is the culture. The culture is what creates the foundation for all future innovation. If you break the culture, you break the machine that creates your products."

Airbnb's culture focused on people showing respect for all of the organization's many stakeholders, not just investors like Peter Thiel, but all of the communities, guests, hosts, and employees who played a role in the company's success. For example, Airbnb developed a "product" called Open Homes after an Airbnb host in New York opened her home to victims of Hurricane Sandy. Her story inspired other hosts to offer rooms to people in need of shelter. By 2018, Open Homes had come to the rescue after ninety disasters around the world. Ten years after its birth, Airbnb's continued focus on creating a culture of "doing good" for all stakeholders helped drive its valuation higher than Expedia, Hilton, or American Airlines (according to *Forbes*).

Consolidating gains often involves people working toward a goal beyond just revenue and profit growth. Do something important, and the money will follow; build a strong culture, and business results will follow. The prescription eyewear company Warby Parker came about when one of the founders, David Gilboa, left his $700 Prada glasses in the seat pocket of a plane in Thailand when he was traveling back to the University of Pennsylvania. He turned up for classes "as blind as a bat" but could scarcely afford the high cost of replacing those designer specs. His predicament sparked an idea for a socially conscious business that would offer that designer eyewear at revolutionary low prices.

Gilboa and three college mates cofounded their company with a straightforward business model: sell in-house designed glasses directly to consumers for as little as $95. If they could do that, they could not only sell a lot of eyewear, they could also provide a lifeline to people whose impaired vision hampered their ability to learn and work productively. This latter goal led the company to establish its "Buy a Pair, Give a Pair" initiative. Whenever Warby Parker sold a pair of glasses to a customer, the company donated a free pair to someone in need.

As of 2018, Warby Parker had donated more than 4 million pairs of glasses through its "Buy a Pair, Give a Pair" program, all the while transforming the American eyewear market with its approach to selling trendy, low-cost designs. Its "doing good" culture resulted in a market valuation of $1.75 billion in 2018, with revenues hovering around $340 million (according to the *New York Times*). Eight years after the company was founded, that's an impressive measure of success.

## MEASURING YOUR PROGRESS

The old saying "You get what you measure" holds true for culture change. While some executives think you can't quantify something as amorphous and hard to grasp as culture, successful change leaders continuously collect and evaluate culture metrics. Three men—Rob Kalin, Chris Maguire, and Haim Schoppik—created the arts-and-crafts marketing organization Etsy in 2005, operating at first out of a small Brooklyn apartment. The idea sprang from the notion that a lot of people would respond enthusiastically to "an antidote to a sea of sameness." Marrying art and culture may seem like a completely qualitative endeavor, but Etsy's founders found a way to quantify their impact on their key stakeholders: artists and craftspeople, art lovers, communities, and, just to make it all harder to measure, the planet.

To accelerate the company's growth, the company brought Josh Silverman on board as CEO in May 2017. Silverman immediately affirmed one of Etsy's key cultural values: "To keep commerce human." This meant offering products that did not come off an assembly line. You want a unique pair of hand-crafted emerald earrings for a girlfriend, a lovely hand-painted ceramic tile for your aunt's birthday, or that leather weekend bag you have been promising yourself as a special treat? Just click on Etsy. Etsy measured and presented some impressive numbers in its 2017 Progress Report:

- Sellers: 1.9 million active sellers around the world generating $3.3 billion in sales.
- Employees: Women making up 50 percent of Etsy's workforce and executive team.
- Environment: 30 percent of global operations relying on renewable electricity, with a power purchase agreement aimed at boosting that figure to 100 percent.

Consider a final financial measurement: Etsy was one of the hottest stocks in 2018, with the company's share price doubling during the year (according to CNBC).

*If you don't measure it, you will lose it.*

With a little creativity and imagination you too can measure different types of culture, and I've given some sample metrics, to help you get started, in the table on the next page (Figure 10.2).

| TYPE OF CULTURE | BEHAVIOR | EXAMPLE METRICS |
|---|---|---|
| Customer-centric | Meets customer needs | Net promoter score, satisfaction ratings, retention rates |
| Innovative | Solves problems creatively | Number of new products launched, revenue generated by new products |
| Agile | Adapts to change | Speed to market, delivery of change goals and milestone |
| Growth-oriented | Works with an entrepreneurial spirit | Business growth rates |
| High-performance | Focuses on results | Net profit, margins, return on investment |
| Employee-centric | Cares about employees | Turnover and absenteeism rates, training investment, engagement scores |
| Disciplined | Abides by the rules | Compliance rates with company policies and rules |
| Quality-focused | Maintains strict standards | Product failures, customer complaints |
| Diverse | Includes and welcomes difference | Age, gender, and ethnicity statistics |
| Safety-conscious | Minimizes harm to all stakeholders | Injuries and safety incidents |
| Sustainable | Meets present and future needs | Energy usage, waste, citations for violations of environmental rules and standards |

Figure 10.2. Hard Metrics for the Soft Stuff

For another example of using a ruler to measure the "soft stuff," take a good look at the financial services firm Edward Jones. According to the firm's website, in 1922, Edward D. Jones established his company in downtown St. Louis in a single room furnished with a desk, three chairs, and a hat rack. Jones wanted to build a firm that involved associates as business partners who fully respected their clients' desire to acquire high-quality investments without paying exorbitant fees. Managing partner Jim Weddle, hired as an intern in the company's Research Department in 1976, maintained those values. For the nineteenth year in a row, the organization was named as one of the best companies to work for by *Fortune* magazine and received an impressive ranking of fifth in 2018. But another number was even more important to Weddle: 0. According to *Fortune*, while the 2007–2008 financial crisis forced competitors to shed employees during the tough times, Edward Jones froze salaries and reduced costs without issuing a single pink slip.

In terms of its internal partnerships, 63 percent of Edward Jones' employees are female. They and their colleagues serve the firm's 7 million investors, not from Wall Street skyscrapers, but in myriad small offices in the cities and towns where the company's customers live and work. To promote service to customers, Weddle developed the Client Experience Index and hired an objective, independent firm to conduct regular client satisfaction surveys. The reports guide the company's efforts to keep its customer-centric culture strong and vibrant.

Leaders can think of culture not as the "soft," relational stuff that resists measurement but as a business dimension that can (and should) be quantified. The extent to which your culture is (for instance) commercial, customer-focused, quality-oriented, innovative, agile, performance-focused, collaborative, or accountable, can all be measured. Once you put metrics in place you can begin see where you need to improve your change capability.

## BUILDING YOUR CHANGE CAPABILITY

I recently heard one CEO say, "Change isn't what it used to be." Like all business leaders, he was facing the tsunami of change sweeping through every marketplace. All those breathtaking new technologies and competitive disruptions and social and economic upheavals make it impossible to keep doing business as usual. The hundred-year-old beauty care company L'Oréal displays a remarkable history of delivering, growing, and adapting. The company's founder, Eugène Schueller, was a French chemist who invented the first synthetic hair color while experimenting in his Paris kitchen. He believed that "a company is not walls and machines. It's people, people, people." That belief led current CEO Jean-Paul Agon to develop L'Oréal's Lead & Enable educational program, which aimed to "foster a new mindset to keep changing its [people's] ways of working." In 2017 and 2018, more than 10,700 L'Oréal managers attended the course.

> *"I am not afraid of storms for I am*
> *learning how to sail my ship."*
> —Louisa May Alcott

This emphasis on creating and responding to change spread throughout L'Oréal's culture, uniting some eighty-three thousand employees in 140 countries, who developed and worked with some thirty-six international brands. Every day, managers would coach their people to get results with agility and innovation, no matter what obstacles blocked their path. To fulfill that mission, the company spends more on beauty research and development than its competitors.

In one notable case, when L'Oréal's research teams wanted to evaluate the effectiveness of its active ingredients and formulas on human skin, they proceeded using biphotonic microscopy to gather three-dimensional information that would show how a product affected the skin. This "virtual biopsy" tested the effects of the company's products without an invasive procedure. L'Oreal builds its change capability by continually experimenting with new ways.

The $54 billion financial software company Intuit (makers of Quicken, QuickBooks, and TurboTax) was also examining its change capability. CEO Brad Smith led the company through eleven years of impressive performance. In 2018, Intuit posted nearly $6 billion in revenue, with a stock price that had increased by nearly 600 percent since Smith took the helm. In an interview with the *New York Times*, he described how he had been a martial arts practitioner since the age of fourteen, and had won a black belt in karate. While teaching karate to 150 students, Smith experienced a life-changing epiphany: "You get measured on the progress of the students you are teaching. It's no longer about your own abilities."

Smith took this insight to Intuit. The company's leaders, he believed, must help their people become change masters. Specifically, they should:

- *Energize*: Get people's hearts beating faster.
- *Educate*: Seize every opportunity to teach and to learn.
- *Empower*: Enable the team to execute after the leader leaves the room.

Smith built the change capability within the company by continually encouraging internal disruptions. The company completely overhauled its Quicken personal-finance software to facilitate online use, made it possible for users to post transactions automatically to Intuit's QuickBooks, and backed 1,400 new third-party apps that strengthened the company's connections with users and accountants. Under Smith's decade-plus tenure, the customer base doubled to 50 million, earnings tripled, and at the time of his departure, return on capital stood at 60 percent (according to the *Wall Street Journal*). In 2018, Intuit was ranked #13 on *Fortune* magazine's list of 100 Best Companies to Work For.

In a fast-changing world you can no longer expect to be able to work with a singular focus. Leaders must move seamlessly from the tactical to the strategic (and back again). They must manage AND lead during times of transformation. The writer F. Scott Fitzgerald put it this way: "The test of a first-rate intelligence is the ability to hold two opposed ideas in the mind at the same time and still retain the ability to function." With that in mind, every change leader should:

- Think like a strategist AND act like a tactician
- Lead AND follow
- Display high IQ AND EQ
- Persevere AND adapt
- Analyze data AND rely on intuition
- Take life seriously AND have fun
- Teach AND learn
- AND so forth AND so on, as you step into the multiple roles required to lead and manage successful change

When you stop learning, you stop growing. And when you stop growing, you stop changing. When that happens, you are at risk of falling victim to more adaptive competitors. You met my client Theresa Martinez in chapter 9. The DressSmart executive found herself in a situation that demanded strong change capability in her team. Although Theresa had worked hard to create an online presence for DressSmart, the digital platform and social media strategy had not generated the new revenue her boss, Svetlana, had projected. Theresa dreaded her weekly review session with her boss. "Svetlana will be concerned about these poor financial results!"

Sure enough, Svetlana made her disappointment perfectly clear. "Without an online channel, we're still not a truly customer-centric culture. You need to get that website humming. If we can't double online revenue in nine months, I will need to seriously review the online strategy."

After the meeting, Theresa asked my advice. "Where am I going wrong?" She looked concerned. "Let's take a step back," I suggested. "Put this problem in perspective. This project requires a team effort. Rather than beat yourself up, think about what the team needs to do to hit Svetlana's numbers. Is Tim in marketing carrying your brand message to ideal buyers? Is Melanie in procurement sourcing the right products for online sales? Is Shana in supply chain delivering those products quickly and efficiently? You may need to improve your ability to work together on this major change, in order to be able to reach your business goal."

Theresa nodded. "I see. We've got to deliver this change as a team, instead of working in our silos. We may need some help to lift our capability to collectively lead and manage this transformation."

With that in mind, she hired a top-notch expert to come aboard and put all of her leaders through an intense "action learning" program. Soon, the team's change capability was making them more changeable, agile, and productive. Revenues from the digital platform began to rise. When the nine-month deadline rolled around, Svetlana called Theresa into her office. "I don't know how you did it, but online sales have almost tripled. Good work!"

When Theresa put both her (and her team's) leadership AND management skills to work on the problem, they got the results they needed. Sure, they encountered a series of obstacles along the way but, by working together, they managed to navigate around these. They were also aware of not slipping back into their old pattern (of working in silos).

## WATCHING OUT FOR THE OLD PATTERNS

As we have seen, culture patterns are powerful, pervasive, and persistent. No matter how hard you try to consolidate your gains, old deeply embedded patterns can easily reappear and pull people back into the habitual way of doing things. BP, the British multinational oil and gas company headquartered in London, experienced the power of patterns during a series of environmental and safety incidents. The company simply could not permanently break an old pattern dating back to the 1960s when BP frequently pursued risky ventures that, if successful, would reap massive profits. Unfortunately this pattern also produced a terrible safety record (according to an article in the *New York Times*).

In 1967, the giant BP-operated oil tanker *Torey Canyon* foundered off the English coast, spilling more than 32 million gallons of crude oil into the Atlantic and onto the beaches of Cornwall. It was an environmental disaster of unprecedented proportions at that time. Almost forty years later, on March 23, 2005, an explosion at BP's Texas oil refinery killed fifteen people and injured 170 others. Three months later, *Thunder House PDQ*, BP's giant new $1 billion production platform in the Gulf of Mexico, almost sank in a hurricane.

In 2009, a new CEO, Tony Haywood, inherited this history of calamities and vowed to make safety "the number one priority." Despite this commitment, the next year an explosion at BP's *Deepwater Horizon* rig in the Gulf of Mexico killed eleven workers and spilled more than 5 million barrels of crude oil into the Gulf. The world's largest oil spill in marine waters created severe environmental, health, and economic consequences that cost the company an estimated $61.6 billion.

Internal investigations into these incidents revealed that senior BP managers knew about these safety hazards but fell under the spell of a culture of cost-cutting at the expense of all else. When Robert Dudley took over as CEO in 2010, he resolved to shift this deeply embedded pattern. According to BP's 2017 Sustainability Report, "In 2017 we continued to see a reduction in the overall number of process safety events, despite a slight increase in tier 1, the more serious events." The whole world hopes BP makes that culture change. However, it will take more than high-minded words to change an old pattern at BP.

If old patterns have worked for the organization in the past, leaders often keep clinging to them, even when the marketplace tells them they shouldn't. Husband and wife Don and Jin Sook Chang, two poor Korean immigrants who arrived in the United States in 1981, built their company Forever 21 into one of the largest fashion retail brands in the world. The Changs' rags-to-riches story whisked them from low-paying jobs cleaning offices and washing dishes to a combined net worth of $6.1 billion in 2017 (according to *Forbes*). The couple opened the first store in Los Angeles in 1984, selling trendy designs for low-priced, disposable clothes to the Korean American community. Before long, other LA teens began flocking to the stores to take advantage of Forever 21's unbeatable prices.

Six years after it was founded, the company had grown to more than a hundred stores, riding the trend toward disposable, fast fashion made by low-wage workers in developing countries. The business model appeared to work seamlessly. Just duplicate runway hits from fashion shows and do it so quickly that your less expensive products would arrive in stores even before the originals. That pattern, however, led to more than fifty copyright infringement lawsuits launched by major designer brands (according to ScienceDirect).

Designers were not the only ones who felt unhappy with Forever 21. Employees rated the company 2.5 stars (out of 5) on the online jobs website Glassdoor (a number much lower than the average 3.3 star rating). They complained about low pay and management's unrealistic expectations. As a result, in 2017, *24/7 Wall St* ranked Forever 21 as the seventh worst company to work for in the United States. Lawsuits and investigations continued, with the Los Angeles Labor Department reporting "significant" violations of federal laws on minimum wage, overtime, and recordkeeping by vendors supplying Forever 21. You can see the old pattern: "We will succeed by skirting the law." It would end up paying for its increasingly tarnished reputation.

A tarnished reputation was also threatening ANZ bank when John McFarlane became CEO and set about shifting its culture in the early 2000s. Seven years later, he had improved customer satisfaction (by 23 percent), created one of the most efficient banks in the world (with a cost-to-income ratio of 45 percent), almost tripled the share price, doubled profits, and significantly increased employee engagement. On top of all that, ANZ had been named the number one bank globally on the Dow Jones Sustainability Index for its leadership role in addressing financial literacy in disadvantaged communities.

However, in 2017, a decade after John McFarlane left ANZ, a Royal Commission into Australian banking skewered the big banks for pursuing profits and monetary gain at all costs. As *Business Insider* reported, "The financial services royal commission identified dishonesty and greed as the main theme from its investigation of misconduct by the banks." The pattern had returned setting back seven successful years of culture transformation. You've got to keep a keen eye on the patterns every step of the way.

## MAINTAINING YOUR ENERGY LEVELS ALONG THE WAY

Culture change won't happen in a week. And often it won't happen in a year. You need to sustain your energy levels for the duration of the change. Treat the journey more like a series of sprints, than a marathon, and look after your own (and your team's) physical needs along the way. Google understood the need to maintain employee energy levels when it applied the "150 feet from food" rule. No one working in Google's East Coast headquarters ever needed to walk more than 150 feet to a cafeteria, microkitchen, or restaurant. That easy access to fresh almonds, dried banana chips, Life Savers, and M&Ms reinforced the culture's emphasis on comforting workspaces.

Some executives I've met work ten hours a day, six days a week, month after month after month, without taking a break to recharge their batteries. Yvon Chouinard, the founder of the outdoor-clothing company Patagonia, rejected the notion that success requires 24/7/365 effort when he introduced the culture's "Let my people go surfing" policy. If you visited corporate headquarters in Ventura on a Friday morning, you could watch people, managers included, ducking out to hang ten at a local beach. Time may not wait for anyone, but neither does the tide. Why let that perfect wave roll ashore without a few Patagonians aboard? The company even posted tide charts above a pile of towels in a corner of the office.

The policy extended to any outdoor activity, from a nineteen-mile bike ride to the quaint village of Ojai, a day rock climbing in Yosemite National Park, or a short excursion to fly fish the Santa Paula Creek. Employees loved working for a company that appreciated the need to recharge your batteries from time to time. As Chouinard often reminded them: "Remember, work has to be fun. We value employees who live rich and rounded lives."

I learned the value of energy management while studying team dynamics as an observer at the Sheffield United Football Club. The football (soccer) players went through cycles of intense activity followed by downtime. After an energy-depleting, ninety-minute game, they would thoroughly rest their minds and bodies. At the end of a long, grueling season, they would take time off to recover their energy and repair damaged muscles. The breaks helped ensure peak performances year after year after year.

It took some serious coaching for Theresa Martinez at DressSmart to learn that lesson. After Theresa's boss, Svetlana, gave her feedback on the new website's dismal performance, Theresa felt like she was coming down with a virus. She booked an appointment with her old friend Dr. Wellington. As she sat in his office later that afternoon, she explained, "We're under pressure at work, with a big change project on the go, which is on top of the usual demands. I've been working late and I'm not eating properly."

Dr. Wellington suggested she might need to look after her health more. "You can't work any harder. You don't need to speed up, you need to slow down. Believe it or not, the slower you go, the faster you'll get there. By that I mean you've got to find a way to manage your stress levels."

Theresa took her doctor's advice and booked a relaxing three-day cruise off the coast of Alaska. When she returned to the office, she set a few new rules: (1) Turn off the iPhone and MacBook from 6:00 p.m. to 6:00 a.m. every day, (2) Get to your desk at 9:00 a.m. and leave promptly at 6:00 p.m., (3) Take every other weekend off to unwind and spend time with friends and family, and (4) Eat healthy, energy-sustaining foods, and get twenty minutes of uninterrupted exercise a day.

Theresa's energy levels steadily rose until she felt like her old self again. Not only did she feel her body relaxing and her health improving, she began to feel optimistic about solving the problems at work without stressing herself to death. As her relaxed attitude and positive feelings rippled through her entire team, the project began to produce results. She learned a valuable lesson. Never again would she compromise her resilience by letting her energy levels get so depleted.

• • •

# REMAINING RESILIENT THROUGH
# THE CHANGE JOURNEY

Culture change is not for the faint-hearted and the journey is full of unexpected twists and turns. Those who prevail possess resilience: They have the ability to bounce back from the setbacks, that they invariably encounter along the way. Steve Jobs, who cofounded Apple in his parents' garage in 1976 was an example of a resilient leader, who had the ability to recover from the knocks he experienced. Nine years after launching his company, Jobs was ousted from the business he had worked so hard to create. But that was only the first chapter in his personal saga of success. In 1997, Jobs returned to rescue Apple from near bankruptcy. By the time of his death in 2011, Apple had become one of the most valuable companies in the world, inventing or transforming whole industries, from personal and mobile computing to the way people immerse themselves in social media and communicate by phone.

The marketplace shifts, presenting the leader with a business challenge—respond to the market demands or face the risk that the business will go into decline. She also knows that the culture must also change, to meet the new conditions in the environment and to unleash the full potential of the business. The change requires courage, dedication, patience, and adaptability. You cannot let the naysayers, blockers, cynics, bystanders, or critics keep you from reaching the outcomes you are seeking. You can't let obstacles, threats, turbulence, and noise keep you from reaching that distant shore. Earlier in this book, we traced the rise and fall of Nokia, the company that once dominated the smartphone industry. Its downfall ruined more than a few stock portfolios. It almost destroyed the economy in the Finnish city of Oulu. Many of the city's 200,000 residents had worked at Nokia's key R&D facility there. When the phone maker sank, 5,000 people in Oulu lost their jobs.

Despite the fact that the city's unemployment rate topped 16 percent, the residents and officials of Oulu applied the Finnish philosophy of *Sisu*, which means "never give up." They launched an all-out effort to tell potential employers all over the globe about the city's wonderfully skilled high-tech workers. The strategy worked. By 2018, Oulu had become a global center for tech innovation in a range of industries that included medical equipment, wearable devices, and driverless cars. In fact, the city became one of Europe's leading "living labs," where residents experiment with new technology such as near-field communication devices used in contactless payments systems and ubi-screens that can turn any surface into an interactive touch screen.

Great leaders never give up on the change vision. Nelson Mandela held onto his vision for a more inclusive and peaceful South Africa despite his twenty-seven-year imprisonment. Arrested and given a life sentence in 1962, Mandela endured backbreaking work in a lime quarry, where the glare of the sun on the white, pebbled stones permanently damaged his eyesight. During his incarceration, Mandela contracted tuberculosis, a disease that frequently made him feverish and fatigued throughout his later life. Solitary confinement, a condition that drove many other prisoners insane, almost killed him.

Yet after a twenty-seven-year ordeal, Mandela emerged from his captivity stronger than ever. Rather than seeking revenge on his enemies, he invited them to share his dream of a better South Africa, where black and white could live and work together in peace and harmony. His leadership forged racial reconciliation and a democratic South Africa—in place of an apartheid state.

Great leaders have the capacity to think beyond today and to imagine possibilities. They are driven by a vision of what can be achieved. Their passion, energy, and resolute focus create a movement that others seek to join. These leaders realize that culture change will not always make them popular, but they put a stake in the ground and lay claim to what they believe in. The courage of their convictions propels them forward on the journey. Like Mandela, the change becomes their driving force and they speak on behalf of the cause, not their ego, which adds to their credibility. Change leaders believe in making a difference in their business and this belief allows them to endure the knocks and setbacks along the way.

Nelson Mandela imagined a South Africa where black and white people could live together with equal rights, and he continued on this quest in the face of persecution and near-death experiences. He did not crumble when confronted with fierce resistance and dangerous opponents. Instead, these threats seemed to make him more resolute in this vision for an apartheid-free country. Mandela never gave up on what must at times have seemed an impossible ideal to those around him. He told his followers: "It always seems impossible until it is done."

•   •   •

## · POINTS TO REMEMBER ·

- The fourth step on The Culture Disruptor is to *Consolidate* your gains.
- With some creative thinking, you can always find ways to measure your progress during culture change.
- Old patterns can easily reemerge.
- It takes an agile and changeable workforce to succeed in a rapidly changing world.
- It's important to maintain your energy levels throughout the change journey.
- True change leaders never give up on their vision to make workplaces better.

# CONCLUSION

## TURNING CHANGE INTO FUTURE SUCCESS

My parents taught me about embracing change as we sat around the kitchen table in our farmhouse in Ireland. "Keep learning," they urged me. "Find your passion; see the world." I did, studying and working in England, the United States, Asia, and, finally, Australia. My parents acted on their own advice, emigrating to Australia in their late fifties and sixties to join their five children (plus grandchildren). When Mom passed away in 2001, my dad moved from Sydney to Melbourne to be closer to me, his eldest daughter. He bought a bright, spacious, two-bedroom, 1960s-style apartment near the shops and the bus stop, where he could catch the 246 bus from Elwood to the Irish Centre in Northcote.

At the age of eighty-eight, Dad fell to the bathroom floor and fractured his spine. Although he recovered well enough to walk again, we worried that his unsteady gait could lead to another accident. It was time, we decided after much anguished thought, for him to consider moving into an assisted-living facility, where he would get the nursing care he needed. We checked out a newly built residential aged-care home not far from his apartment. With less resistance than I had imagined, Dad put his name on the waiting list.

Four months later, the facility called to say that a room had opened up for him but that he must move into it within the week. When I asked him what he planned to do, he finally showed a little resistance to the idea. "I'm not ready to move just yet. I need new socks."

The situation reminded me of much of what I had learned about culture change over the years. Old assumptions are hard to alter; old patterns are hard to break. Here was a man who had lived an independent and active life and had always thought of assisted-living facilities as "old folks homes," where frail and feeble elderly people spent their twilight years. That was not a role he could easily accept. But if he replaced that assumption with a new one, accepting the fact that he had reached the point in life where assisted living made sense for him and his family, he might enjoy playing a new role as an aging father who could continue to enjoy his life and his family free from the medical worries that beset all of us toward the end of our lives. He did just that. Before the end of the week, he had made his decision. "I'll do it. It makes sense for all of us. I'll give it a month. If it doesn't work out, I can always go back home."

My dad needed to let go of the independent ways, that had served him for so long. And here he was, instinctively applying the change skills he had learned through traveling the world for work when young, emigrating to Australia from Ireland, and nursing my mother through illness. He had questioned his old assumptions, reframed his role in life, and shifted his behavior accordingly. He moved into his new home and never looked back. He loved the residents and staff, and they loved him. On my regular visits, I often found him singing "Galway Bay" or reciting a W. B. Yeats poem to an audience of elderly ladies. He lived happily in this community for several years before he died peacefully there, his hand holding mine.

The lesson my father learned was how to let go of the old ways, that had once worked for him. In organizations, these old ways have worked for you, on some level, otherwise you would not be here today. My ex-boss and former colleague John McFarlane certainly learned this lesson. As John prepared to leave a decade after he had begun building a more "human" culture at ANZ bank, I hosted an event to celebrate the successful transformation. The bank, no longer a toxic and bureaucratic place to work, had won the admiration of employees and customers alike.

I wanted the event to be a global festival. We invited employees from all corners of the business to submit ideas that encapsulated what the bank's culture meant to them. More than five thousand people responded and submitted entries to the culture festival, in four categories: art, photography, short film, and song. We shortlisted finalists in each category, who most powerfully depicted what the bank's values meant to them, and invited these employees to showcase their entries at a gala night at Melbourne's Festival Hall—with hundreds of ANZ employees in attendance.

As John McFarlane walked into the venue, he found himself in the midst of the arts category finalists featuring paintings, photographs, and sculptures that depicted the bank's culture. John chatted to Amara from Bangalore, who had taken a photo of her elderly father looking into the lens, because his face reminded her of the bank's value of integrity. Later that evening, we watched the films and heard the songs ANZ's people had created for this special occasion. I saw John listening intently as a Maori choir from New Zealand performed a rap song about the bank's value of diversity. The short film category was next and the CEO watched a short animation, created by David, a bank manager from the rural town of Dubbo. It told the story of an office worker who had felt trapped in his job but then decided to break out of his old ways by thinking differently about his work.

The festival turned all those hard-to-grasp aspects of culture into powerful symbols of the remarkable change at ANZ. At the end of the evening, John wandered among the guests, saying his farewells. People milled around him, eager to shake his hand, thank him for the positive difference he had made in their lives, and wish him well in his next role. John McFarlane not only understood the need for change, but made it happen.

Most organizations operate in a fast-changing environment requiring leaders to constantly adapt. An organization's culture often must adjust to meet the changing business landscape and customer demands. Continual change can present exciting opportunities for those who have the know-how to transform workplace culture into a source of competitive advantage.

The Culture Disruptor contains the four key steps necessary for any business facing culture change, as the organization pursues a workplace that can deliver, grow, adapt, and continue to prosper.

Throughout this book, I have explained and illustrated how The Culture Disruptor can help individuals and organizations cut through the challenges of culture change in four relatively straightforward steps (see Figure on the next page):

- *Diagnose* what's really going on in the workplace and beyond,
- *Reframe* the roles of different parts of the business,
- *Break* the deeply embedded patterns, and
- *Consolidate* their gains.

The Culture Disruptor provides a proven way to transform culture, with lessons sourced from my thirty years' experience—much of it as an "insider," in charge of culture transformation in large organizations. Along with the supporting analysis in this book, it is designed to help you wherever you happen to be on your culture change journey. The Culture Disruptor can assist leaders continue to be successful, help those who are struggling with specific culture issues, or support more radical workplace change.

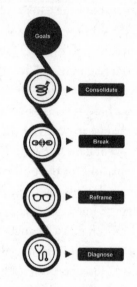

The Culture Disruptor

On any culture change journey, always keep in mind what's central to workplace culture. Contrary to popular opinion, culture is less about the explicit values and behaviors, and more about the mental maps, roles, and patterns. Dealing with these key elements of culture will give you the greatest leverage during any culture transformation.

In fast-changing marketplaces, bosses face the challenge of adjusting the culture to meet the shifting business landscape and increasing customer demands. This continual change can present exciting opportunities for those who have the know-how to transform workplace culture into a source of competitive advantage. Culture change can be extraordinarily rewarding, but it can also be challenging. Remember, the journey may require you to give up the ways that once made your organization successful.

# INDEX

# INDEX

# INDEX

# INDEX

# INDEX

# ABOUT THE AUTHOR

**Siobhan McHale** has worked across four continents, helping thousands of leaders to create more agile and productive workplaces. She also has been on the "inside" as the executive in charge of culture change in a series of large, multinational organizations. One of these inside jobs was a radical seven-year change initiative at Australia and New Zealand Banking Group Limited (ANZ) that transformed it from the lowest-performing bank in the country into one of the highest-performing and most admired banks in the world. Professor John Kotter used her work with ANZ as a Harvard Business School case study designed to teach MBA students about managing change.